How to Leave a Group Chat

Thank you for buying my book! Please leave a review on Goodreads!

How to Leave a Group Chat

Louisa Guise

The Book Guild Ltd

First published in Great Britain in 2024 by
The Book Guild Ltd
Unit E2 Airfield Business Park,
Harrison Road, Market Harborough,
Leicestershire. LE16 7UL
Tel: 0116 2792299
www.bookguild.co.uk
Email: info@bookguild.co.uk
X: @bookguild

www.louisaguiseauthor.com
Twitter: @whatiwrote_
LinkedIn: Louisa Guise

Typeset in 11pt Minion Pro

Printed on FSC accredited paper
Printed and bound in Great Britain by 4edge Limited

ISBN 978 1835740 026

British Library Cataloguing in Publication Data.
A catalogue record for this book is available from the British Library.

To the one-and-only Smartie Monster, my Nanna Mary Lubas. I dedicate my first book to you to say thank you for a million trips to the library, for never being able to pile me with enough books and for every time you said to me "you could write a story about that". You always knew this day would come, even though you didn't live to see it.

Well, now my name is in print and so is yours.

Contents

Introduction

"These [people in the group chat] are people I see and talk to regularly, although the bond in the group is not as strong as it used to be. But it's been like this for nearly two years. A couple of times I left it and immediately got the separate messages 'what's up' 'is everything ok?' 'Why did you leave?' I'm sat over here like BECAUSE NO ONE IS REPLYING!!! But I'm the weird awkward one for trying to leave a group that won't communicate. If we were all sat round a table in the pub, and I asked the same questions it would be really frigging awkward if everyone ignored me (which I'm confident wouldn't happen in real life) so why so rude on WhatsApp?" (littlemisseatsherfeelings, 2016)

First, human beings communicated with spoken words, body gestures and other vocal noises. Then came a different kind of communication as we began to use tools to etch, draw and write, a means whereby we could communicate with each other without being physically present. We had now worked out how to communicate remotely. This distance grew over time with the invention of new communications, of the radio, the telephone, television, and computers. With computers came not only the ability to connect to and communicate with other people remotely, but the means to do so within the confines of a constructed virtual world. As this virtual world developed alongside more mobile technologies, we became even more present within it. Through social media we developed the ability to construct new digital identities for ourselves and to fully communicate with each other there, immersed as this new persona or avatar. Social media has radically changed communication as we know it, as well as who we are now communicating with and how often. It has heavily influenced how we engage with each other, on our smartphones and in the real world, in more ways than we could have ever imagined.

Instant messengers and social media are still a relatively new way through which we can socialise and communicate. They have become a normal tool in our everyday lives, although the ways in which we use them do not always make sense from an evolutionary point of view. We have sleepwalked into using this new communication and, despite having become very experienced in using it, many of us are still not entirely happy or comfortable with this new technology. For example, we might feel annoyed when a friend keeps glancing at their phone when we meet them for a coffee (despite the fact that we might be guilty of having done exactly the same thing in the company of someone else) or we might feel stressed as we feel compelled to answer an instant message right now even though we know that we really have to leave the house so that we are not late for something important.

We do not only use instant messengers to communicate one-on-one. Pretty much all of us who use instant messaging apps are part of a group chat, and very likely not just one. My first instant messaging group chat involved a group of friends from my hometown on a very purple app called Viber before one by one we gradually made the switch to WhatsApp. It felt like group chats and WhatsApp groups came out of nowhere, because all of a sudden there were many of them on my phone, each serving a different purpose. I had groups chats for different friendship groups both near and far, with colleagues across different jobs past and present and for family (once my parents finally worked out what to do with WhatsApp). I have been added to groups to arrange holidays, parties, hen dos and to keep up with a yoga schedule. Like any conversation, at first the instant messaging group is always fun. It is nice to be included in a group chat with friends, family, or colleagues, whether you know them well or not. It is a thrill to have someone you can always have on hand to chat to at any time of day, or to share a funny joke with the moment that you hear it. But like any conversation, the conversation in the WhatsApp group can run its course. Instead of coming to a natural end, the chat is still on your phone, and so are all the other chats that you are part of. Like littlemisseatsherfeelings above, you might have difficulty leaving a group chat even if you really want to.

Why someone might want to leave a chat should not really matter, yet it is common for participants to worry that the other participants might conjure up all kinds of reasons for their departure and they do. It is rarely perceived or acknowledged that someone in the chat wants to leave because they simply want to leave the chat. Why is it the case that other participants sometimes worry, or take offence, when someone leaves? Why would the people that littlemisseatsherfeelings talks to be so determined to bring her back into the group chat?

This was the catalyst for writing this book. I have been a communications professional (under the various guises of content writer, digital marketing manager, communications lead and similar) for over ten years, yet the etiquette around instant messengers and social media has fascinated me since it started to infiltrate my life as a high school pupil. I can remember, aged twelve, when MSN Messenger was set up on the computers in the school computer room for the first time. Some pupils were already using it at home. Everyone was excited and adding each other to their contact list and for that brief hour the social hierarchy that existed between my classmates did not apply. Children who would normally never show any interest in me were asking for my email address so that they could add me to their account. Why would the kids who never spoke to me want to have conversations with me via this virtual platform? I have the unique perspective that most of my childhood was free of mass multimedia communications, and I was still quite young as they began to be a daily occurrence. In both my personal and professional life, I have observed how they have bloomed and how our behaviours have changed along with them.

Carry out a simple Google search and you will realise that lots of internet users are asking for advice on how to leave or manage group chats across blogs, newspaper articles and in internet forums. Many users appear to be stressed. A lot of their worries are only based on what they think that everyone else will think. Yet despite the fact that there are so many concerned app users, I have not come across another book which solely addresses this subject – until now.

The focus of this book is on instant messengers and how people behave when they use them. Through looking at communication, how it has evolved and how we communicate differently in different dimensions, this book aims to help us make sense of the group chats in which we communicate and seeks to demystify some of the ways in which group chat participants might behave and explain why they might behave in the way that they do. Through doing so, the book will look at what has previously been individually assumed by group chat users and help you understand these assumptions. WhatsApp will be mentioned a lot because it is one of the most dominant chat apps at the time of writing, and the most frequently used among my friends and family across Britain as well as in many countries worldwide (this fact is nicely demonstrated by WhatsApp being called the heart of the smartphone by a recent UCL study that we will discuss later in Chapter 4). However, WhatsApp is not the only programme which allows you to maintain a group conversation. The issues and topics covered in this book will apply to any chat app that has this function. Facebook, Snapchat, WeChat, Viber, and others all allow you to chat to multiple users at the same time. This function is very popular and shows no sign of going away any time soon.

Introducing the Chapters
In the first chapter, A History of Group Chats, we will look at the history of group chats and learn how they became

what we know and use today. We will discover how and why they transcended from being on large, slow, bulky machines to featuring on tiny devices that fit in the palm of your hand. We will chart the evolution of the devices that host group chats and the institutions that created them. We will discuss this because, although technology is not solely responsible for dramatically changing how human beings communicate, there is no doubt that without these developments we would not have radically altered how we communicate and dramatically changed our behaviours as a result.

Chapter 2, Communicating in Different Dimensions, will follow this by explaining how different methods of communication work and how they have evolved over time to function between people across greater and greater distances. These different types of communication are categorised under different dimensions, a term which describes communication according to how it functions and where it takes place, whether that is in the real world, whether it bridges the gap between two or more people during space and time, or whether it takes place entirely in a digital world. These communication dimensions have been labelled the First (real-world communication that takes place in close proximity to other people), Second (grounded in the real world but able to communicate over longer distances via apparatus such as a telephone), and the Third (communication takes place entirely in a digital world) dimensions. Each of the different dimensions exists in relation to the technology that exists or has evolved over time. The chapter explains why this is important to understand and ends by describing how the different dimensions can be crossed as well as the behavioural changes that have arisen within each dimension as we have adapted to them.

After explaining the different ways in which humans communicate, we will look at how discussions in the real world compare to discussions in online chats and apps. Chapter 3, How Group Chats Work in Real Life and in the Virtual World, will focus on the mechanics of how conversations and human communication work, highlighting the differences between how humans communicate with each other in-person and how people communicate within the digital world in more detail. It discusses how group chats work in the real world (by this we mean conversations that take place in-person between groups of people in the same room). This is important to discuss because before we communicated with the addition of any kind of aid, we communicated using our own bodies and sounds, and this is still the starting point for all of our communication and something which when it is absent, we miss more than we even realise, however much we might enjoy playing with new technology. The chapter defines what a chat is and the conventions surrounding conversation. It then moves on to discuss how people converse via an instant messenger and how this differs, or might be similar, to how human beings would converse outside of the digital realm.

Chapter 4, The Positives and Negatives of Group Chats, explores how instant messenger group chats play both a positive and negative role in our lives. The first part of the chapter focuses on the positive things that are associated with participating in a group chat including how instantly important information can be shared, the social bonds that can be initiated and strengthened and the source of support that it can provide. The second part discusses the negative aspects of partaking in group chats, including the absence of communicational markers that we have evolved to rely on as humans. As we will see, this absence has led to some very interesting changes in behaviour and ultimately it is at least partially responsible for the fact that we end up locked into conversations that we no longer have any interest in participating in, or perhaps did not want to be part of in the first place. We will find out why.

Chapter 5, Grouping Chats, delves deeper into the world of group chats. There are different types of group chats that exist on instant messengers in the Third Dimension, and we discover that not all group chats are the same. Despite having similar functions and overlaps, group chats can serve different purposes. There are many types of chats that could be explored in detail, however, the family chat, the friendship group chat and the work WhatsApp groups are the ones that are discussed in more detail here, because they are good examples to represent a number of important factors and issues that are common across different types of chats. The family chat was chosen because it is made up of people with whom we have the strongest bonds, and it is where we act out our most defined roles. Being part of a chat with relatives (sometimes more than one chat with various assortments of family members) can impact on, enhance, and even strain the relationships that we have with those relatives.

The discussion about friendship group chats uses the term friend in the broadest sense, acknowledging that the chat might not just be made up of any one person's actual friends, but a spectrum of people, from those who they may know to friends of friends and people who might just be in a chat together because they happen to live near each other. Friendship bonds may fluctuate throughout our lives and the chat can impact different friendships in different ways, strengthening them, weakening them, erasing them, or all of the above.

The work group chat has been widely adopted in the workplace, although, you might be surprised to learn, some messengers such as WhatsApp do not officially permit their messaging apps to be used for business purposes. These chats can be both a hindrance and a help. A group chat can allow you to send important messages to colleagues quickly (which, as we will learn in the next chapter, is why it was developed in the first place). It can also blur that important boundary between colleague and friend which can lead to its own problems in a professional environment. The work group chat could just be one of the least-wanted chat groups due to the fact that for many, its very presence can prevent people from truly switching off from work.

By assessing different types of chats, this chapter aims to further help develop an understanding of group chats by highlighting some scenarios and theories which might help you see the medium in a new light. There is not a huge amount of literature in existence that deals with group chats in this way, so I will draw on personal experiences as well as experiences of others that I have come across both through discussing the topic of this book with people close to me as well as online during the course of my research.

Now that we have developed an understanding of how communication works, how it has changed, the good and bad sides of group chats and how different types of group chats work, Chapter 6, Chat Etiquette, can establish some written rules for group chat users. Some are basic good manners such as asking people if they would like to take part in a group chat before adding them, remembering to keep the conversation relevant and to discuss topics that are suitable for everyone involved. Others are about maintaining self-control such as discussing arguments elsewhere and not taking anything too personally. As well as learning how to behave within a group chat, this chapter has some good tips for real-world behaviours that can also help you be a better group chat participant such as limiting smartphone use, changing the colour of the phone to greyscale so that you are not so compelled to use your phone and getting into the habit of using the broadcast function to message many people at once without obliging everyone you are messaging to be in a group chat together. We will explain why these rules and techniques are important, how they can be achieved and how they can help you.

Leaving the WhatsApp group and how to do that is a fitting topic for the final chapter and what the book works up to. The chapter begins by talking about choices and discusses the act of leaving the group chat. The act of leaving is physically easier than the drama which surrounds it, and the next section discusses what to say before leaving a chat and how to deal with the aftermath once you have left. It talks about how other participants might react so that you feel prepared for this and then provides some helpful technical steps to prevent yourself being added back into a group chat. At the end of this chapter, you should feel more capable to let the conversations interfere with your life less and instead work on those relationships that mean the most to you by engaging with the individuals you care about in solo conversations and in the real world.

Finally, we will conclude by summarising everything that this book has taught us. After reading this book, you should come away empowered to take part in as many or as few group chats as you want to, for as long as you want to, and to exit each chat when you are ready without any uncertainty or guilt.

Chapter 1

A History of Group Chats

In this chapter we will look at the history of group chats. Originally, when humans and computers communicated, there was only a two-way dialogue between a single user and a single computer. Instant messaging services changed that. The medium itself has a short history, which is still longer than you might imagine, and it even predates the internet. In this chapter we are going to take a whirlwind tour through sixty-one years of the instant messenger's development, learning more about how instant messengers benefited man and machine, and how they gradually became incorporated into, and infiltrated, our everyday lives.

In the Beginning

Let us begin with something that may be familiar to many (of a certain age). AOL Instant Messenger (AIM). Internet provider America Online's (AOL) instant messaging service was originally attached to the AOL browser, but after being launched as a separate entity in 1997, it rapidly grew more popular to become a staple method of communication well into the noughties. AOL may have been the first time you had ever heard of an instant messenger, and the little yellow running man logo has become as recognisable as the McDonalds golden arches. However, this is not where the story begins (Gregersen, 2020).

Like many other modern technological marvels, instant messaging is said to have begun at the Massachusetts Institute of Technology (MIT), a university in Boston. Among the institute's many achievements, MIT is world-renowned for advancing the development of computer science. It was here that some of the earliest interactive video games like Spacewar! (a war game where combat takes place in space) were programmed and where the World Wide Web Consortium standards organisation was founded. In 1961, one hundred years after MIT was established, the Compatible Time-Sharing System (CTSS) was developed at the institute's computing centre, which was the predecessor to the instant messengers that we know today.

The CTSS was initially developed to speed up how quickly computers could receive and process instructions. Early computers received instructions from punch cards which were manually inserted into a machine one by one. The term 'programme' refers to a collection of instructions that can be given to a computer. When lots of instructions, or a programme, were fed into a computer to process at the same time, this became known as batch processing. Once the programme had been fed into a computer, the Central Processing Unit (or CPU – the brain of the computer) of that computer would process each instruction in turn whilst a magnetic tape recorded this. After a few hours the programme would be ready and then it would be taken to another computer and manually inserted in order to complete the next step.

Although by the early 1960s computers had advanced from running one instruction at a time to a programme at a time, they were still slow and inefficient. The latest CTSS now featured a main messenger that was hosted on a central computer called a mainframe. Users would input instructions into the mainframe via remote terminals which, unlike the computers we know today, were typewriter consoles fitted with electronics. The CTSS also featured a master programme called a supervisor programme which timed each instruction and then instructed the system to move onto the next user in turn. This new system was fast enough to get through all of the users who were using the system at the same time whilst also providing a visibly continuous service at each of the individual consoles (Museum, 2010).

Technological explanations can be hard to follow, so here are a few essential terms:

Compatible Time-Sharing System (CTSS): A data processing method which allows users working on different computers to access the same information at the same time.

Programme: A collection of instructions for a computer.

Batch Processing Technique: When lots of instructions are given to a computer at the same time.

Central Processing Unit (CPU): Also known as a central processor, main processor or just processor. This is the computer's brain. It is the section of the computer than retrieves and executes instructions.

Mainframe: A giant supercomputer which other computers are connected to. Essentially a large brain that is shared by multiple computers.

Programmed Logic for Automatic Teaching Operations system (PLATO): A mainframe-based computer developed by the University of Illinois, originally intended for educational purposes.

Supervisor Programme: A programme which times each instruction and instructs the system to move onto the next user.

Remote terminals: Essentially these are electronic typewriter consoles.

In 1963, twenty-one consoles could connect to the mainframe and the instructions that were inputted directly into the system could be processed in seconds. By 1965, several hundred universities were engaging with the CTSS.

One of the First Instant Messengers

One of the earliest computer systems to feature an instant messaging system is the Programmed Logic for Automatic Teaching Operations system or PLATO, a mainframe-based computer developed by another acclaimed American university – the University of Illinois. As the name suggests, this machine was developed for educational purposes and many different versions of PLATO emerged throughout the 1960s and '70s. PLATO is hailed for being ahead of its time as it was the first generalised computer-assisted instruction system and it introduced brand new computerised concepts such as plasma display screens (remember, before this, computers were technically modified typewriters), touch screen input, interactive graphics, and electronic mail (e-mail). During the early 1980s, PLATO systems were incorporated into a number of desktop computers, including those produced by big computer manufacturing companies including IBM and Atari.

The Seventies

By the '70s, the potential for instant messengers was growing. In 1971, the instant messaging system featured as a chat function on a government computer network of the United States Office of Emergency Preparedness, with the aim for information to be exchanged quickly during emergencies. Known as the Party Line, it was intended to replace telephone conference calls. Users would log onto the same computer via a phone line and then read the text on a screen. Like the later instant messengers that are more familiar to us, the Party Line displayed a list to show who was participating in each conversation (it allowed a maximum of thirty participants to take part) and alerted users when someone left or joined the group. It was used on a device called the Teletype Unit which the Morechrome Kleinschmidt Corporation (later renamed to the more punchy and popular Teletype Company) had been manufacturing since the 1930s. The Teletype machines, which were like a typewriter, fax machine and printer in one, had become particularly popular with businesses and news stations during the Second Word War, due to the fact that they could receive news quickly, and they were eventually also adopted by the American military.

In 1973, David R. Woolley created what is credited as being one of the first online message boards – PLATO notes for the PLATO system. In the same year, one of his fellow students, Doug Brown, created Talkomatic for PLATO, a programme which allowed several users to converse through text as a group, when he was just seventeen years old. Talkomatic is credited as the first instant messenger because it allowed users to participate in virtual group chats for the first time. You can try out a more modern web recreation of Talkomatic for yourself, also created by David and Doug, at

https://talkomatic.sjzoppi.com/lobby.html.

Later in the '70s, instant messaging software became even more accessible with the launch of Talk on UNIX operating systems (UNIX being the system behind Linux's and Apple's operating systems' façade, the equivalent for Windows was MS-DOS). Talk is a programme known as a daemon programme, that is, a programme that is always running in the background (on Windows operating systems, a daemon is known as a service). Talk allowed users to copy messages from their computer terminal to the computer terminal of another user and when they did this, pop-ups appeared on the recipient's computer to alert them that they have a new message. All a user had to do in order to contact another user on a different terminal was input their username as a command. An incorporated programme called Finger told users if their friends were online or not and gave user details such as their real and login names and when they were last seen online. Talk still runs on Linux computers today.

Before we come to the era of the World Wide Web in 1989, or even before computers commonly featured a graphical interface, the Bulletin Board System (BBS) was used to exchange messages or files across virtual networks. If you are not old enough to remember this system, the most famous example in Britain, and many other countries, is the Teletext system that featured on televisions in the 1970s through to the early 2000s. Teletext was a static service which could be updated from the back end, but the system also offered the opportunity to talk to other users. It could be argued that that it was the precursor to the internet as we know it, and it is not hard to see why. In the early 1980s, message networks on the BBS such as FidoNet featured a service similar to modern email called NetMail.

Messengers of the Nineties

We now return to AOL Instant Messenger, which was incorporated into the AOL web browser before coming into its own in 1997. As the popularity of AOL grew, it was inevitable that other instant messaging services would be developed. ICQ (I seek you) came along from Israeli company Mirabilis in 1996, to be bought out by AOL just two years later. It was followed by Microsoft's MSN Messenger in 1999 and Nordic instant messenger Skype in 2003. These were just some of the names to become mainstream. Although Microsoft had already created NetMeeting, one of the earliest video call programmes in 1996, Skype was the real game changer because alongside featuring text chats and the capability for group chats, its main focus was video calls. In May 2006, the service had the ability to include up to one hundred participants in the same call (DSP, 2021), effectively realising the dream that Talk had a couple of decades earlier to evolve the conference call. Skype was widely adopted by businesses conducting remote tasks, as well as by ordinary people who wanted to keep in touch with each other over longer distances.

The Unholy Trinity: Device, Social Media and Instant Messenger

Despite being quite a technologically advanced piece of software, it is easy to forget that what instant messengers do is actually quite basic. They serve two simple functions: to monitor if users are using the app in the here and now (and to alert other users to their digital presence), and to allow users to send messages to each other. They might not be so interesting and have become so central to our lives if it were not for two other things: the technological devices on which they are held, the smartphones, or social media, a tool which instant messengers have combined with in a big way and owe much of their popularity and social conventions to. Instant messaging services stood alone until social network MySpace incorporated a chat function in 2006, with Facebook following suit in 2008. These developments are significant because it is social media use that began to pave the way for mass communication on such an impersonal level. Social media websites are platforms that serve the sole purpose of allowing us to promote ourselves. They are essentially online forms that encourage us to reveal as much information about ourselves as we can, to connect with others – our virtual friends – and in turn to encourage our virtual friends to reveal as much about themselves as they can. As we are not physically present on this site but only virtually present, we can lose many inhibitions that might ordinarily make us more private and guarded individuals and as a result many social media users behave in quite a narcissistic way (more on this in Chapter 4). A consequence of having so much personal information about any one person readily available is that when engaging in exchanges of communication via social media, we do not have to make as much effort to communicate, because a lot of what we might talk about and what we might learn about other people is already known. We are now placed in a digital dimension where #hashtags can fill in unspoken gaps that we did not even know were there and GIFs and memes can replace our own words because we already know the main things that might have filled our conversations. All we have to do is click Like or share a hundred posts that have now become opinions of our own. Now, the instant messengers and social media sites have merged, meaning that these behaviours can transfer seamlessly from social media to instant messaging app.

However, at this point in time, although our behaviours may have changed, a person still had to be on a desktop computer, connected to the internet (at this point most of us still largely relied on a wired internet connection), and logged into their respective MySpace or Facebook account in order to be contacted via the chat function. This was all about to change. The mobile phone as we know it changed forever when Apple launched what was arguably the most revolutionary new type of telephone to date in 2007 – the iPhone. This new-generation device transcended the phone from the simple speaking device that we one once knew into an entirely new gadget that we know as the smartphone. The humble telephone had now turned into a tiny computer which incorporated a phone with a camera, photo album, games console, web browser and more. It had the capability to connect to the internet via its own 2G data network. It was this ability to connect to the internet, along with the ability to add functional applications or apps, that allowed smartphone usage to snowball. Former Yahoo employees Brian Acton and Jan Koum were inspired by this new technology to create the messaging app WhatsApp. As WhatsApp evolved, each new release was updated accordingly in order to make the most of the iPhone's new features, such as push notifications (Wikipedia, 2021), or as they are more commonly referred to, pop-ups.

Not to be outdone by WhatsApp, Apple launched iMessage in 2011. Apple's new messaging app was intended to replace text messages, which had been widely available on phones since the launch of the first Nokia in 1993 (Arthur, 2012). iMessage improved the regular text message (which was, as its name suggests, just messages containing text) by allowing users to send everything from text and emojis to photos and files. Instant messaging services on mobile phones were not only a hit because of their technological advances; they also proved popular because text messages cost money, and messages sent via these services were free (or in the case of WhatsApp initially, substantially cheaper – the app did charge a small fee until 2016). iMessages are free between users of Apple operating systems, but other than that, no matter which operating system you are using on your smartphone (or desktop or tablet for that matter), it is possible for many users to be part of the same conversation when they use an instant messaging app.

Boom. Social media instant messengers complete with their group chats were now on the smartphone. We now have access to social media and instant messaging chats twenty-four seven. The slot-machine design of the smartphone façade, with its bright colours and noisy notifications, is no accident, and social media was already shaped to maximise consumption. Facebook founder Mark Zuckerberg's degree was in Computer Science and Psychology, and he has designed the platform in a way that makes it very hard to switch off. We are able to send out targeted messages to multiple people at once, even to people we have never met, and these recipients in turn are able to respond instantly – and they do, for exactly the same reasons that we are contacting them. As this technology has become increasingly used on pocket-sized devices that we always keep on our person, the behavioural changes that have become established through it such as indiscriminately contacting others, willingly baring all and putting ourselves on show have become even more pronounced and commonplace.

Since WhatsApp and iMessenger, newer apps Snapchat, Instagram, WeChat, TikTok and Telegram have also been added to app stores, but not before other desktop messengers and websites had released messaging apps of their own with Skype and Facebook also eventually featuring on smartphones in the form of apps. The list keeps growing as the latest incarnations of instant messengers hit the app stores. Despite the fact that instant messengers were initially developed to assist businesses with their communications, by the early 2000s, it was not long before they had become part of many people's lives, and in the subsequent years they would become part of many more.

Chapter 2

Communicating in Different Dimensions

Like every single species on earth, human beings have always communicated. Our communication is shaped by the design of our own bodies, the environment that surrounds us and the tools which we have to hand. As the tools of communication have evolved, the way in which we communicate has evolved too. To help illustrate the differences between the different types of communication, I have termed each the First Dimension, the Second Dimension, and the Third Dimension. The First Dimension is when we communicate with spoken works, bodily gestures, and other vocal noises. The Second Dimension, which came next, is when we etch, draw, and write – it is when we are able to communicate without being physically present. The Third Dimension is when we communicate within an entirely new realm altogether: the digital realm. By categorising different types of communications in this way, an understanding is gained of how human communication has evolved and in turn we can see where there might be conflict between the way in which we naturally communicate and how we adapt our communication for each dimension. These adaptations, which are in relation to both different technologies and the growing distances between people, can create a potential for a conflict as we juggle how we naturally want to communicate and the restrictions that each dimension places on our means of communication. Read on to learn more about each of these communication dimensions in greater detail.

The First Dimension

The First Dimension is a term that refers to any communication that happens in-person within the same space where there is nothing blocking or carrying the conversation over a distance. The same space is defined as any area where two or more people are or are able to be physically near each other and in turn they are able to observe the person communicating as they communicate. The important thing is that they can experience first-hand the conversational markers that indicate not only what someone is saying but also how each person is feeling or what they might be thinking. These can include things such as a person's voice, tone of voice, sign language in the case of deaf speakers, facial expressions, body language and so on.

The First Dimension definition applies when two or more people are conversing to each other, whether quietly next to each other or whether they are shouting to each other from a reasonable distance. A reasonable distance is not defined by a precise length, however, it is a distance in an environment where two people are able to be in close proximity to each other with little delay or few barriers; for example, a reasonable length can apply if two people are shouting to each other from different rooms in the same building. It applies as long as they can hear each other's voices even if over a bit of a distance. Two people stood at the opposite ends of a field can still hear each other's voice and tone of voice when calling to each other, even if what is being said might not be so clear, and there will be other indicators that show what they might be trying to communicate such as their body jumping, waving arms, or pointing. Two people within the same household might shout to each other from different rooms, but their tone of voice will be clear and other noises such as creaking floorboards or the clank of other items can assist the speaker in conveying meaning, even if the two people speaking to each other are not visible to each other. At least one of them has to be able to move to be near the other person quickly.

In the First Dimension, the voice is not carried by technological means. There are disabled people who might communicate with the aid of a computer because they cannot communicate using a biological voice. As they are unable to use their own voice, the apparatus used to assist them fills in the role of their own voice but does not carry their voice over a distance like a telephone would. These disabled people will be communicating in the First Dimension as long as the above criteria – that they are either present in the same area as others talking to them or they are able to be present before those communicating to them with little delay, or anyone who is calling to them is able to be present before them with little delay – applies. The same is true of anyone who is conversing with someone else using a voice alteration device. Sometimes, when many people are together, someone might use a megaphone or Tannoy to communicate clearly to multiple people at once (such as at a school sports day or to make announcements in a supermarket). As long as the person or people carrying out the act of communicating are within the same area as the other people they are communicating with, or are easily able to be, this can also still be defined as First Dimension communication. In this scenario, the sound of the voice alteration does not mean that people conversing cannot see each other. Anything else that is present when people are communicating in the First Dimension merely serves as a prop and does not mean that the participants are communicating in a different dimension. Non-verbal props such as photos, printed texts or slides may also be used in conversations that occur within the First Dimension. Whether communication evolves across distances or is carried out much closer, human beings are excellent storytellers and love to use additional means to bring their story to life, no matter how communications evolve or how far apart the communications occur.

The communication no longer happens in the First Dimension when the conversational markers mentioned are no longer present, or the people conversing are not able to physically be near each other. All parties involved just have to be within a close enough range that if they are not in the same space, they are able to be within sight (or a distance that would allow people to see each other in the case of those with no sight) of each other within a very short space of time (less than a few minutes). Any further apart and you are now communicating within the Second Dimension.

The Second Dimension

Communication in the Second Dimension occurs when you can communicate with someone else without being physically present, either actively or passively. One of the earliest examples of this would be cave paintings which were, amongst other things, a method of conveying information to someone who might visit the same cave after the person who had written the information was no longer there. Like the imprinted and printed items that came after cave paintings, (such as stone tablets, hieroglyphics on pyramid walls, books, leaflets, newspapers, billboards, etc.) information was provided by absent people to people they may or may not have ever met. A cave person entering an empty cave could learn from the markings on the stones inside where to pick the best berries, the way to the nearest source of water or simply be entertained by the heroic story of a great man defeating a fearsome beast. A person's sense of where they were was not altered by this information or the way in which they received it. The person in the cave is still in the cave just as the child reading a book in bed is still in their bed. They are aware that another person not too different from themselves has written the information before they had arrived at that place, and they knew that others would see this information after them. The cave-dweller might even have added to the information that is present or amended it so that it is more helpful when the next person finds it.

Later came technological advances that allowed people to communicate actively and at the same time from a distance: the telephone, walkie-talkie and the two-way radio, and passively: the radio, the projector and the television. The telephone allowed people to communicate verbally in different locations at the same time, yet there was no denying that each speaker was in a real world location, most likely in their home. A person's voice sounds slightly different over the receiver than it would normally sound if two people were speaking face-to-face in the First Dimension, but the difference is slight and the voice still recognisable. Over the telephone you can gauge the pitch and tone of someone's voice and from this know relatively accurately someone's emotional state or their health, even if their voice is not exactly the same. You get to know their telephone voice. As most landline telephones are kept in a single location, and they do not feature hundreds of apps and a web browser, there is little else to distract a speaker from what the other is saying, and if there is a distraction, that distraction is grounded in the real world, such as a pan boiling over or the dog trying to jump up on the sofa. The distraction is not another function on the telephone device. Each speaker is grounded in their own physical location, and although they might be able to picture the location where the other person is speaking in their mind, they are not absorbed into another world.

In the Second Dimension, it is possible for more than two people to converse at the same time, especially via the telephone because more than one landline telephone can be connected in the same house on the same line at the same time. Later, conference phones allowed multiple participants to converse over the telephone together through dialling into the same conversation via different telephones that were not located in the same place. These are still used in offices around the world today, although digital software such as Microsoft Teams and Zoom have largely taken over this role.

The passive technological advances such as the radio, the cinema screen, and the television are all one-way communication and included in the Second Dimension category because they do not involve individuals communicating in the same area but rather, like the cave paintings, involve recordings of communications in time, whether a time in the past or live in real time. Both radio and television broadcasts can be live, and the viewer appears to be addressed directly ("If you want to win a trip to Ibiza, ring us on [number] and answer this question.") but indiscriminately as there is little scope for them to respond directly to the person addressing them. Some viewers might respond by messaging or ringing the television or radio show to answer a question or to contribute to a debate, but only a fraction of the viewing or listening audience will actively be able to do this. Interestingly, it is a common habit for listeners and viewers to respond directly to the radio or TV without directly talking to anyone involved with a television or radio show ("Yes I love this song", or "He's talking rubbish") even though the person on the end has no idea that they are doing so and does not know who any of the viewers are. Even pets such as dogs and cats have been known to respond to certain stimuli on the television or radio. Dogs in the real world have been known to bark at dogs that are themselves barking on television programmes.

On television and on the big screen there is body language. It is (in most cases) fake or improvised because the people who are recorded are acting and animated. However, regardless of whether the body language is genuine or not, the viewers can still relate to it and derive meaning from it. Even though the body language is visible, this is still Second Dimension communication because the subject is far away, and the viewer cannot reply via the use of their own body language. Although they cannot make contact, they can, however, respond with physical responses such as, for example, putting their hand over their mouth when they see something shocking. This differentiates television from a Third Dimension communication such as a Skype or Zoom camera call where the other parties can respond to someone's body language using their own body language in real time.

It is possible to be immersed in a television programme or film in the cinema in the sense that you will concentrate fully on the media playing out in front of you. Cinema, with its darkened room, is possibly the more immersive medium of the two because the lack of light in the room cuts you off from the other people in the same space and ensures that the moving picture on the screen in front of you is the centrepiece and where your attention will be focused. However, the passive nature of the film playing in front of you, and the fact that you are isolated from the others sitting around you, prevents you from becoming fully immersed in a new world where other people can also be fully immersed with you in real time. Each cinema goer has their own unique experience when watching a film, and a similar effect is also possible should you choose to dim the lights at home and watch a film on the television together in silence. How engrossed you are with any film or television programme also depends how much you like what you are watching.

The Second Dimension is an in-between means of communication. Either you intend to leave a message, such as in the example of the book, cave painting or billboard, and not physically meet the person you are interacting with, or this means of communication fills in the gaps and you have an intention to communicate with the person you are communicating with in the First Dimension eventually (and probably soon). Someone you ring by telephone is very likely someone you also see in the real world. You do not intend to remain within the Second Dimension within its own right and retain all of your communications there, as you might do in the Third Dimension.

The Third Dimension
Communication in the Third Dimension happens when exchanges of communication take place within a constructed virtual world. This shared environment is immersive. No party is physically present in the same space, but everyone taking part shares the same virtual space such as the instant messaging chat box or an immersive video game world. Due to the fact that the entire conversation happens in the virtual realm, the

essential markers of communication which are always present in the First Dimension such as someone's voice, tone of voice, sign language in the case of deaf speakers, facial expressions, body language and so forth are often missing. This means that in the Third Dimension it is easy to lose the context of communication and there is less indication of how someone is feeling and what they might be thinking.

Even though the environment of the instant messaging chat box or app might be rather bland in appearance, it still constitutes a very immersive virtual space, and whether the conversation takes place within a plain chat box or a more animated video conversation, a lot plays out within each conversation. The virtual realm that the conversation participants inhabit can be made all the more real by sharing virtual items in real time or when the participants all become avatars within the virtual world of a video game. Communication in the Third Dimension happens within this constructed world. It happens in real time, or at least always has the ability to within the lifespan of the particular immersive virtual space. You might not respond to a group chat the instant that a single message is sent out, but there is nothing in the app to stop you from doing so; if anything, you are encouraged to do this.

Social media websites like Facebook and MySpace share a lot of features with Second Dimension communications, such as books and cave paintings. What sets them apart and allows them to be defined as Third Dimension communication mediums is a couple of things. Firstly, on social media we construct an identity and, as a result, complete this image of ourselves by adding information that fits into our digital persona. We become literal Facebook friends, interacting with profiles that have become an online persona of us rather than bonding with the people behind the profile. Not all of the information on any given profile is necessarily true or accurate. How often have you seen umpteen photos of two people on a social profile, two supposed besties, only to meet one of them in person and have that person complain about that other person the entire time? Or how often have you seen pictures of someone smiling in a group at a family party, before you meet that someone in the real world and they complain about everything that was wrong with that supposedly perfect day and how annoying certain relatives were? The information we provide on our personal social page is selected to fit with how we want to be perceived digitally and, paradoxically, by knowing more about a person, we might actually know them less.

These social media sites are also always 100% accessible to their users who can interact with each other in real time whenever and wherever they are, with notifications popping up as the interactions take place. For example, consider the following fictional scenario:

Lowri is in Cardiff at her best friend Jenny's hen do. It is 10pm and the stand-up comedy has just finished. The comedy club is being transformed into a disco for the rest of the night and the hen party is just getting started. To thank everyone for an amazing day, Jenny, dolled up to the nines with a sparkling sash to match, has placed a tray of prosecco on the table. The bottle sits in the middle of a ring of ten glasses. Lowri, overcome with joy, leaps out of her seat, and calls to Jenny to pause as she begins pouring prosecco into the first slim glass. She zooms her phone in onto Jenny's perfectly manicured hands and taps the screen with a click, and then again, following the bride from different angles as Jenny pours, pauses and poses. It does not take long before Lowri has several photos to choose from. With another tap, the best photo – the one where Jenny's engagement ring and glow-in-the-dark nail polish gleam under red lights – is uploaded to Facebook.

Lowri's phone buzzes and so does Jenny's – she is tagged in the photo which means that even more Facebook users can see this image in their profile. Notifications pop up on the home screen, causing both their phones to light up. The comments are instantaneous and along the lines of:

"OMG lush!"

"Hope you're having a good time."

"Don't get too drunk!"

And so forth.

There are not many pings from the pop-ups before both Lowri and Jenny are on their phones and in the Facebook app, liking the messages and replying in real time with such messages as:

"Thank you hun! xxx"

"It's amazing! [very excited smiley face emoji]"

You get the idea.

As is demonstrated in this example, the Third Dimension features communication alerts which instantly announce to a user that they have been contacted. This is very different to the simple yet persistent ring of the regular telephone which lets recipients know that they are being contacted right now but they will only be reached if they are at home. Pop-ups appear on the smartphone screen, accompanied by pings, the second that a message is received. Even if the message is sent on a site such as Facebook and you could realistically look at it tomorrow, one or both of these notifications will catch your attention and it will be hard to resist. There is even an announcement to alert you to the fact that someone is typing as they type. The Third Dimension conversation metaphorically leaps out of the self-contained virtual world and through your smartphone screen. The default setting for pop-ups is to contain a snippet of the conversation, to entice you to read it, of course, and even if you have changed the settings to anonymise these notifications, the ping or the buzz of a phone ensures that it is very difficult not to log into the platform in question and check the messages. You will be replying to your messages pretty quickly. At first glance this probably seems like the biggest difference between communication in the Third Dimension and communications in the Second Dimension. In the Second Dimension, it is easier to leave a message and look at it later. This, however, is not strictly true. Even prior to the smartphone, it was not always easy to ignore a telephone that was ringing or to put letters to one side to open later. The big difference is that we are almost always aware of the moment when we receive a communication on a smartphone and that this moment of awareness is no longer brief because the smartphone is both a complete portal harbouring multiple communications at the same time, so the list of things for us to check is ever growing, and it is never out of sight or out of mind. Once the regular landline telephone has rung, the moment to check who rang fades quickly, and it is easier (although not easy) to put letters on the table and read them later than it is to ignore instant messages. The smartphone is also where we will almost certainly receive the most exciting information. Letters and answering machine messages – which were where we once learnt about important things such as being hired for a new job or whether someone had passed their exams – are now messages conveyed mostly in the Third Dimension. I do not know about you, but the only people I ring now are utilities companies and the only letters that pop through my door are bills. The boring stuff.

Conversation in the Third Dimension is varied and consists of multiple types of media such as photos, videos, web links and voice clips. We have already mentioned that these media elements can be added to conversations in the First Dimension as props to support a conversation and bring a story to life. However, in the Third Dimension they shape the virtual world rather than enter a conversation as a separate entity and can strongly indicate a lot more than what is being said by verifying a statement (whether correctly or falsely) or highlighting an emotional state. Hashtagged words are the equivalent of words, thoughts and emotions being conveyed in 3D – they metaphorically pop out of the screen and have entered into conversations in their own right. #Yestheydid #itstrue.There are a lot of human elements missing from conversations in the Third Dimension which have already been mentioned. As well as hashtagged words also conveying extra information (#angry, #happy, #sad) a common feature of communication in this dimension is that elements such as emojis, and actions such as hugs, written between asterisks (which often embolden due to the formatting settings within chats) are added to conversations. Although it is very difficult to imagine Third Dimension conversations without emojis, they are nothing new. Emojis began life in print, and even transferred to handwritten letters, as combinations of printed characters such as:

:) [smiley face]
;) [winky face]
:([sad face]

In this older form, these more primitive emojis still served the same purpose as the emojis that we know today – to compensate for the fact that these very human elements or emotion are missing from the letters and other correspondence in which they featured. As the technology has evolved, so have emojis. There are now even custom emojis which can be created as a cartoon image of the speaker, blurring the line between avatars and these conversational markers further. The meanings conveyed by these additional elements complement the conversation but are not always related to the conversation itself and all are contained within this virtual world.

Crossing Communication Dimensions

One of the best voice messages I ever received was when a friend's mother rang to see if I had taken home an item by accident after a horse riding trip. The conversation went something like this:

"Hello this is R here, H's mother. I was just ringing

to see if Louisa has taken my riding boots by... [voice alters as R turns to tell off child 1]. D! D! Don't touch that. [Returns to the call with a very polite tone] I'm sorry, my son was being naughty. As I was saying... [voice alters again as two children are shouted at]. No J! J! Leave him alone! D, stop fighting... [Returns to the call with an ultra-polite tone] I'm sorry, one minute. [Friend's mum tells her children off. What is said is not entirely clear, but it is very funny to listen to.] [Returns to the call with a polite tone] I am so sorry about that. Please give me a ring on [number]. Goodbye."

As this conversation beautifully illustrates, conversations and communications do not always take place solely in one dimension or another. The phone call example detailed above shows how a conversation can take place in multiple dimensions at the same time and cross that divide. Here my friend's mother was communicating simultaneously in both the Second Dimension (over the telephone to us) and the First Dimension (in the hallway to her children). It is very common for two or more conversations to be happening simultaneously with any number of participants once the conversation crosses dimensions. Participants communicating across more than one dimension at a time will still only be part of one conversation at a time within each dimension. They might tune into more than one conversation for a short time but will quickly choose one or the other. Although the regular telephone is not a smartphone, in this example my friend's mother was not entirely present when talking to us in the Second Dimension, nor when disciplining her children in the First Dimension, and in the end, she had to make a choice between the two dimensions in order to communicate to both of us over the phone and to her children in the hallway effectively. In this case, she chose to leave the Second Dimension conversation with us (or rather, our answering machine) temporarily in order to have the more immediate First Dimension conversation with her children, before returning to the Second Dimension conversation to finish the objective of trying to find her riding boots.

This particular voice message from my friend's mother was recorded long before smartphones came into existence, and the conversation would not have been too different had someone from my household answered the phone and responded to her in real time. Yet one could equally imagine the same scenario with a mother speaking into the receiver of a regular telephone also with an iPhone in hand, typing away into an instant messaging app and shouting at her naughty children without looking up. The smartphone is designed to occupy our attention and its constant presence means that we are more likely to only be partially present in a First Dimension conversation, as we find it harder and harder to direct our energy away from those Third Dimension conversations. This can affect real world relationships, as people are increasingly only partially present with others sitting next to them. The act of ignoring those you are near in the real world is so common that there is a new word to describe this phenomenon – phubbing, which as of 2021 has entered into the Oxford English Dictionary. Had she held a smartphone at the time, my friend's mother would almost certainly have communicated less effectively with both us and her children. Many times, I have had friends give me half answers as they stare at a device messaging someone else and I almost certainly have been guilty of this too, although I try hard not to do this around other people. I once observed as a child was scolded for running off without telling their parent where they were going when they had in fact done their best to ask for permission to play 'over there'. In the moment that they had tried to ask for permission, their parent was glued to a smartphone and only muttered a vague response to the question without looking up or really having heard what their child had said. Knowing that their parent was not communicating with them and that they probably would not get a quick answer, the child took matters into their own hands and went to play 'over there' anyway, despite also knowing that there might be consequences later.

As for applications like Microsoft Teams and Zoom, where do they fit in? Again, we communicate in the virtual space, yet this time we can see the people speaking right in front of us. We hear their voices – which sound more accurate than they do over the telephone – and we can respond to them in real time. In a sense, we cross the dimensions digitally. We could even go as far as to say that this communication takes place in another dimension – the Fourth Dimension. I anticipate that these messengers are a precursor to the metaverse and hologram communications, new forms of communication that are still in their infancy but apparently coming soon. What does seem to be agreed, is that conversations that take place over Teams or Zoom do not provide the same level of human satisfaction as communicating with others in the First Dimension.

Then we come to events such as parties and get-togethers, which are usually full of different clusters of people engaging in conversation. This is not always comfortable for everyone, and we have probably all been at an event where we did not really know anyone and making conversation with total strangers was an awkward and terrifying thought. This is when the smartphone can be a godsend, a means to be present without being present. The common complaint now is that all people do is play with their phones instead of attempting to interact with anyone else nearby. This is negative because if someone is with you in the real world, they should be engaging with you and not with someone else remotely. However, the smartphone has become the semi-acceptable way to be alone in the corner without trying to engage with anyone.

How acceptable this action is depends upon how well other people know the person who is in their own world on a smartphone instead of taking part in the event fully. People who do not know that person well would be less concerned, people who are closer to them might be more annoyed. If too many people in a room were to stare at their smartphones at the same time, nobody at the party would interact with anyone else and therefore it would not be much fun and no host wants that. In taking the action to invite someone to an event, the expectation is that the guest will be present and participate, but the reality is that the guests will likely be navigating different dimensions of communication throughout the day.

What is also much more common is people becoming so absorbed in the digital world that they take video calls or flick through Instagram with the sound on without any consideration for anyone else around them. It is hard to tell if it is no longer considered rude to disturb others with your personal noise, or if other people are just afraid to speak up.

Privacy is also being eroded. On a recent trip to Naples on a crowded pavement in the centre, a man was taking a video call in front of me, shouting into his phone. As the crowd became tighter, he held his phone up above his head and the entire street could see that the friend he was talking to was in the shower, rubbing shower gel into his body as he spoke! In an even more recent trip to Orléans, France, a couple in the pool and sauna area believed they had the right to watch sport on their iPad in the pool and the Novotel staff told me they couldn't do anything about it when I complained. It will be interesting to see how these communication dimensions, and our behaviours within them, evolve in future.

Chapter 3

How Group Chats Work in Real Life and in the Virtual World

Human beings are intelligent. We have used this intelligence to design and develop ways to communicate using tools which have in turn allowed us to communicate from greater and greater distances. Some are simpler tools like pen and paper, and some are more complex apparatus such as telephones and computers. However, despite these great advances, we are still human beings first, mammals who have evolved to communicate within the world in which we originated, using the bodies into which we were born. It is this communication within the First Dimension which forms the base of all human communication. As we communicate in each successive dimension, we adapt our communication in order to work with the tools at hand. We also adapt our communication to match others so that we are not left out. For example, my accent subconsciously changed a number of times when living in different countries to make myself more understandable and I dropped some of the heavy Britishisms so that my friends, a large number of whom spoke English as a second or third language, could understand what I was talking about. It is important to consider how we would communicate in the First Dimension when discussing these subsequent adaptations because communicating in the real world is when we communicate with each other in our most natural state, and it is only through understanding this that we can understand the context in which we communicate in the Second and Third Dimensions and why we might act or feel the way that we do as we communicate. As we cannot use all of our natural communication methods within each dimension, we lose some of the elements that are vital for us to understand each other and connect with each other. This can be very problematic, but, as we will discover, it can also work in our favour.

How Group Chats Work in Real Life

Whether you are at home, on the street or at a gathering, every conversation starts with two people. It makes no difference if you are in an intimate setting such as at home with family, a formal setting such as in an office or an informal setting such as a party, the chat becomes a group chat when others decide to join in. Anderson and Myers say that there is consensus that a minimum of three participants equals a group (Anderson & Myers, 2008) and this seems sensible, anything less is just a two-way conversation. If a conversation is being held in an area where many people are present, others could be listening to your conversation, but they are not part of the group chat until they are actively participating in the conversation itself. In Chapter 2, I gave the example of my friend's mother who was juggling two conversations in two dimensions, and the same principle applies within a single dimension – eventually each person will choose one conversation and give it their full attention in order to communicate effectively within it.

Most conversations happen organically, with willing participants joining, taking part and speaking at will as the moment seems right. Other conversations are prearranged, such as a more formal meeting between parents and teachers at parents' evening at school, during a Q and A session after a talk, or at an established occasion such as a funeral or work conference. Wherever a conversation is held, planned or spontaneous, participants decide to take part because they may be aware of what the chat is or will be about, the chat is interesting and relevant to them, or, if prearranged, the conversation may be necessary, such as to discuss your child's bad behaviour at school. A conversation can be formulaic, random, or predictable, or all of these at once. A formulaic conversation can start with a greeting, perhaps introducing yourself or your companions, asking how others are, flowing through into the main point of the conversation and ending with a goodbye. Any topic mentioned can influence the next topic. Random topics can occur when one participant might interject with something that is on their mind, comment on something unexpected that is happening near them or say something when the conversation reaches a pause that needs to be filled. A conversation can be predictable when you know someone well because you might correctly guess how they may respond to a particular topic, and even if you do not know them well the mention of subject A could very likely mean that you are both now thinking about subject B because that topic evokes shared cultural associations, or it could be a topic that has recently been at the heart of gossip or a subject in the news. Each conversation can come with different rules and rituals depending on who you might be talking to, and these may change as the conversation progresses, becoming formulaic, predictable, and random at the same time as the number of participants taking part in the conversation increases, or decreases as participants run out of steam.

Cues and Conventions

The circumstances in which the conversation is held, whether in a formal or informal setting, can influence the topics of conversation. In addition to this, the physical location of the setting where a conversation takes place dictates to an extent what might be spoken about, with linguist David Crystal going as far as to argue that in an arranged or more formal setting "notions of social decorum and appropriateness outrank other considerations" when choosing a topic of discussion in conversation (Crystal, 2020). For example, at parents' evening, parents and teachers would engage in a respectful discussion and mostly stick to a limited selection of topics such as how the child is performing in school, how well they are achieving in different subjects and how the child behaves towards staff and other pupils during the school hours. There is not much scope for personal chit-chat or political opinion. At a funeral it would not be customary to say anything about the deceased that is not nice, and perhaps you would not show off about that very expensive car that you just bought or laugh loudly at something hilarious that happened. You would be polite and quiet and give words of condolences or comfort.

As well as abiding by any cultural conventions that would apply to events such as funerals and parents' evenings and the physical settings around us, we take cues from other people in order to guide how we communicate, paying close attention to what they say and how they act. All of these aspects come together to form a complete frame of reference and we alter our communicative behaviours accordingly. A conversation with a neighbour on a bus might be lighter chit-chat, perhaps about surface-level things that we have been doing or small talk about the weather; a conversation at a wealthy Christian friend's perfectly decorated home might be kept proper and conservative; here we might mention that we met up with some friends at the weekend but might not delve into the details of all of the ungodly things that happened on that particular occasion. By contrast, a conversation with a very good friend when sharing a bottle of wine might have no limits or morals.

Beyond the Words - Conveying Meaning

Body language directs the way in which participants converse. "In ordinary conversation up to as much as 70% of all communication between two or more individuals is delivered though body language," (Valentino, 2016) with some studies suggesting that the amount of conversation communicated via body language and tone of voice could be as high as 93% (Mehrabian, 1971). Facial expressions can tell the people who we are talking to if the story we are talking about is funny, sad, annoying, or factual, and, as long as the participants in the conversation have understood correctly, they will react accordingly. A funny story might be replied to with another funny story. If you tell a story whilst looking annoyed or sad, the person you are speaking to is unlikely to laugh or reply with a funny anecdote. They might express sympathy or a shared annoyance. How personal the information is that you share, and how detailed that personal information is that you share, will be dictated by these factors. It will also be determined by how well you know the person or people that you are talking to. This is illustrated by the fictional scenario below which compares how you might give the same information about the same event to a best friend versus to a colleague:

[**Telling your best friend about something annoying that happened at work.**] I was in a meeting with my team and our top client, and my line manager was so rude. He kept interrupting me when I tried to put forward my solution. And he arranged the next meeting right when I had scheduled a dentist appointment that he knew about a month ago. He did this even though the client suggested that they could do a few different dates! Now I have to get a new appointment and there isn't another for two months! I'm so annoyed with him! *Argh!*

[**Telling a colleague from your team about the same annoying thing that happened at work.**] The meeting with our top client went okay and we seem to have found a way forward for the project. The annoying thing is that we're having the next meeting when I had arranged a dentist appointment, so I have to reschedule that which isn't the easiest thing. Oh well.

To further indicate meaning, we adjust our tone of voice to precisely emphasise each of the words that we say. Tone of voice can convey how you are feeling very accurately, give your listeners a sense of a character (e.g. someone impersonating their mother or demonstrating a different accent), a more accurate description of a scenario (e.g. "He shouted at me, 'Oi, you in the green trousers!'"), or provide more insight into how the speaker is feeling. In order for people who are part of a conversation to acknowledge a speaker and build rapport with them, they will face the person talking and possibly position their body closer to them. They will nod, make eye contact, and interject with backchannel responses such as, 'yes', 'uh-huh' and gasps. Both the person speaking and the others who are part of the conversation will be paying close attention to everyone else's responses and reactions because how people react to one topic can determine the next topic that will be talked about. If the other participants did not seem interested when you spoke to them about football, you might not continue talking to them about sport, but if everyone was very engaged when you told them a funny story about your childhood, you might tell them another story about your childhood.

"A good conversationalist will notice and acknowledge when a conversation has run its course. Some of the signs that indicate boredom and distraction can be: fixated eyes and an unwavering head… Forced smiles… Jiggling feet, tapping fingers, checking the smartphone… doodling." (Kuhnke, 2016.) It is important to keep tabs on other people's reactions in order to foster and maintain good relations with them. If a conversation no longer interests your fellow participants, the subject of the conversation should be changed, or the conversation should end and the participants should not be made to feel obliged to stay. People will generally try to avoid anyone who they fear might trap them in bad conversation.

How Long Is a Conversation?

The length of any given conversation is as long as a piece of string (even conversations that are supposed to have time limits, such as a meeting or other event, can naturally overrun or finish early), but what is certain is that the conversation will end. The same conversation might transfer between different individuals who enter and leave it at various points, but even so it will eventually end. People will be part of the chat until the end and eventually the chat will have served its purpose. Burtis and Turman argue in Group Communication Pitfalls Overcoming Barriers to an Effective Group Experience that the purpose of a group conversation is the most important aspect of a conversation. It should be shared between participants because "if group members are working towards different ends, they will only appear to be a group until their desire for different things results in efforts by them to separate their activities" (Burtis, John O.; Turman, Paul D., 2005). This is why a one-sided conversation, such as one that would involve one person talking about their favourite subject non-stop with few pauses, does not work. This type of conversation means others do not have a chance to join in or change the subject, and this leaves the speaker alone in their desire. In this instance, everyone else who is involved in the conversation will feel uncomfortable and intend to leave the conversation as soon as they have a chance to.

Once the conversation has been exhausted, or when something else requires attention, people may leave, perhaps turning to talk to someone else, by turning their attention to something non-verbal such as a television that is on in the corner or the book in their hand, or by physically removing themself from the vicinity. Usually, before moving away a person will excuse themselves, either with a genuine reason or an invented excuse. If many people are part of a conversation, participants can easily leave without a reason, sometimes at the same time. A person may be able to re-enter the conversation at any point in time if it is continued by other participants, however, no one is obliged to be part of the conversation and there is an undefined limit (but a limit nonetheless) as to how long the conversation can last.

How Group Chats Work in the Virtual World (The Third Dimension)

Someone somewhere in the world decides to initiate a group conversation, the group chat. This could even be a joint decision between two or three people together in the same vicinity, or a decision made by a couple of people virtually, but it takes one person to create the chat room and invite others. As everyone is using the same social platform, the door is always open to whoever wants to make contact, whenever they might want to make contact or not. No one is left out. Based on the rule of three (Anderson & Myers, 2008), the group chat is officially set up once at least two other participants are added in addition to the host. Due to the technological capability of the instant messaging app, the participants who have been added are then able themselves to add new participants. It can often happen that participants can be added to a new group chat unexpectedly and without their permission being asked first, as the example below shows:

"My phone was pinging away from 9pm. I stopped the work I was doing to see what exciting messages from a dear friend might be awaiting, only to discover I'd been added to a work WhatsApp group?! Too thrilling were the exchanges that I would not bore you with the details, but there was nothing that could not have been conveyed in an email. But of course I now have to either put up with the tedious banter or do the very public 'screw you' and exit the group." (Allthebiscuits, 2019.)

Just like the Mumsnet member above, you can suddenly find yourself as part of a group conversation on a messaging app that you may or may not have asked to join. The likelihood is that you were simply added, and that no one had asked your permission first. You might know the person who set up the group chat, or another of the participants in the conversation, however vaguely. However, equally, in the case of a group chat set up on an instant messaging app to arrange a hen do or a birthday party, you might not know the person who added you or even anyone else in that conversation.

The Missing Cues
In a group chat conducted entirely via text, body language is absent, and do not forget that we could rely on it in

order to deduce up to as much as 93% of the meaning of a conversation. Whatever the precise percentage of communication conducted via body language, there is no doubt that in any conversation where you cannot see a person's face, body movements, distance, or posture, or hear their tone of voice, you are going to miss vital cues that determine precisely what their words mean.

In conversations that take place in the First Dimension, it is possible to ask for clarification or to explain a misunderstanding, and someone in the conversation is highly likely to notice the misunderstanding and point it out. Misunderstandings are more difficult to notice when conversing over an instant messenger in the Third Dimension and any doubts are often expressed privately, rather than to the group. To try and compensate for the lack of body language, emojis are used to convey a smile, frown, or shoulder shrug, as are added explanations (e.g. "When saying this I do not mean X but actually I mean Y") and spellings adjusted to convey an accent or colloquial way of speaking (e.g. "How yo' doin'?" or "Whazzup sista!"). The hashtag symbol is also used.

The hashtag, which is historically a symbol that represents a number, is something which, in a digital context, originated in code to highlight specific parts of text. As we have already mentioned in the previous chapter, today it is used to add feelings or an emotion to a statement, compensating for the lack of conversational cues, and it leaps out of the screen in a similar way to the thought bubble rising from the head of a cartoon character.

E.g. Hurrah I got a new job #madeupcompany #yay #excited #newjob #job.

Hashtags are another trait that became part of popular culture via social media and instant messaging discourse. As well as conveying emotion or side thoughts, the hashtag is still used to group social messages across all platforms into topics. It was adopted by Twitter (now known as X) users to group tweets and allow users to find tweets related to a topic such as #jesuischarlie after the Charlie Hebdo attacks, #MeToo for the Me Too women's rights movement and #BLM for the Black Lives Matter movement.

Despite using tools like emojis and hashtags to compensate for the lack of human elements in conversations, the full meaning of communications in the digital realm can be confused or lost because there is no way to make up for something as fundamental to our understanding of each other than the cues we get from each other when interacting face to face. Without a full, and shared, understanding of each other, participants frequently assume their own conclusions. It does not help that a consequence of human intelligence is that we often overthink things that happen to us. This tendency to overthink, coupled with the absence of the essential communication markers in the group chat, can give us too many interpretations of any given scenario and as a result, lead us to reach incorrect conclusions about what someone might have said, or even something that they might not have said. It is also possible to reach incorrect conclusions about what is said in conversations that happen in the real world and this can happen for a number of reasons. However, in most cases this is much more difficult to do when we have full access to all of the conversational markers that can only be provided when we talk to others face to face.

The Chat Box

In the Third Dimension, the conversation that happens in group chats takes place within the realm of the chat box. The chat interface itself is not a physical location. Because there is no physical setting such as a friend's familiar living room, a doctor's clinical surgery or a church decorated to the nines for a wedding to act as a point of reference and give additional cues as to how a conversation should start, progress and end, or how we should conduct ourselves, we improvise by inventing our own rules for communication. Physically changing settings is in itself one way to ensure that conversations do not last too long. Knowing that participants can leave is one way to ensure that those conversing are kept in check and that the mental health of participants is preserved. How many times have you had a conversation in a pub or a living room with a group of people and then left the area to go outside and get some air or to talk to someone else? For some people conversations can be exhausting and, as human beings, it is normal to change our surroundings. A never-ending group chat in the same digital space could become claustrophobic, akin to spending too much time stuck in the same room, especially when there are studies to suggest that the average conversation between two people would only last approximately thirty minutes (Cooney, 2020).

Every chat on an instant messenger has a similar set-up, with a bar at the top with the participants' or group's name, the main body of the screen hosting textual messages displayed in frames representing speech bubbles, various media (e.g. videos, photos, audio files) and a white strip along the bottom where messages can be typed via a tiny on-screen keyboard. In this sense everyone participating looks ambiguously the same. Everyone is constructed of text, as a collection of pixels. The chat interface allows us only to communicate through a limited number of actions and blocks the aspects of communication which make us human. Group chat participants can now be ambiguous. This ambiguity of the digital world allows people to hide any anxieties or insecurities that they might have in the real world. Take the example of Amy:

"Amy barely says a word to boys at school or a party, but she rushes home to talk to them online. There, Amy says, you can 'take a breath', relax, and plan what you are going to say before sending your message. In-person, a conversation can get out of control, go flat, or stop dead. Online, Amy feels playful.

[Amy's response.] "If you have a relationship with a person, you think they're cute and stuff, you can make more of a conversation online than you would be able to in-person because when you're in-person, you're intimidated by the person. You like them. You do not know if they like you back. Online, you can say 'hi', and they'll say 'hi' back, and you can start a full-blown conversation. In-person, there are so many reasons why you do not want to talk to that person. Because you think, 'maybe they think I'm ugly' or something like that."

Given these anxieties, when she is having a face-to-face conversation with a boy, Amy tries to keep things short and then get him online as soon as she can." (Turkle, 2015.)

In the Third Dimension there is no need to worry about how you look and what you are wearing, because behind the safety of the smartphone screen no one else has to see this. The digital conversation also allows you to plan what you might say beforehand or to construct an image of how you want others to perceive you, but it is much easier to lose sight of how your habits, mannerisms and actions might come across to others. The entire character of the chat is defined by the participants' interactions and the meaning that can be interpreted from them. As we have already mentioned, multiple individual meanings can be derived by different participants from the same words that one person has typed. As a result, what should or should not be off limits is arguably more ambiguous. We rely much more on the typed words and other media in order to decipher how we should conduct ourselves in each conversation.

Can You Be the Judge?
Without the essential verbal and visual clues such as body language, it is also much harder to judge what is appropriate to talk about, how long to talk about it for and if anyone in the chat is interested in what you have to say. Add the instantaneous nature of the instant messenger to the mix and you can see why at the height of a group conversation, or any Third Dimension conversation, participants frequently submit messages and other media to the chat without giving a second thought about what they are conversing, why they are talking about a topic or how what they want to talk about might come across to other people. It is too easy for a person to offend others in the chat, and in the same vein, if a person constantly bores other participants with an exhausted or uninteresting

topic, they might not be aware of this. In response, instead of giving the essential cues that participants might give if they were talking face-to-face, participants might not respond at all. This might indicate to the speaker that their topic is not of interest, or the silence could be interpreted as the other participants are not available to respond at that moment. Whatever the real reason – and each group participant might have their own – often the loquacious speaker will continue to flood the group with comments and media about the same topic (e.g. their new baby or new car) because it is something that interests them. Participants in the group chat might respond with positive comments out of politeness, however vague or neutral, or to keep the peace between friends. If there is no obvious disinterest shown, those participants will receive more communications about the same subject. It could also be the case that one or two other participants could be genuinely interested in or like the topic discussed, and as they are the only one or ones to express this, the speaker has the green light to continue conversing about this topic. The uninterested parties might be groaning or pulling faces behind the screen, but the speaker has no way of knowing this. The unwelcome conversation can cause underlying annoyance for uninterested participants who, if they were conversing in the First Dimension, would have found a way to change the subject or perhaps just left the conversation long ago.

Participants in group chats might not just talk about the same subject too much, they might talk about something too personal and overshare. "Oversharing, by definition, is 'too much information' [abbreviated as TMI] – the posting or promulgating of highly personal information, such as one's relationship status." (Agger, 2015.) What is considered highly personal is open to interpretation and may depend upon not only how well you know the person but how close you are to them. Typical topics that could leave other participants feeling negative (guilty, at a loss, repulsed, embarrassed or awkward) could be anything personal, of a sexual nature, nudity, or a deep insight into one's mental state (such as details of a psychotic episode). If participants in a group chat know the person who is oversharing well, their close bond could mitigate some of these negative feelings, possibly even turning them into feelings of amusement ("Ah he's going on about that again!") or sympathy. If the other participants in the group chat might not know you incredibly well, they might not feel comfortable to be told the intimate details of your divorce or hear about what made you cry. People by nature are also copycats. When they see others behaving in a way, such as sharing certain subjects, they have unwritten permission to do the same and they do. Social media has made oversharing okay, and it was not such a problem when you could choose what to engage with. It is much harder to be selective when the subject is being shared directly to you and not to a webpage that you could choose not to look at.

A large number of people engaging in the same behaviour also removes any taboo about that behaviour and this has become the case for oversharing. However, despite taboos about group behaviours lessening, the fear of upsetting the group is ever present. All of the participants in a conversation are present in the virtual chatroom for the entire duration of the conversation whether they chose to be or not, or whether they are actively participating. Participants in a group chat will only cease to be a part of the chat if they decide to leave – and leaving can be the hard part. Unlike when you might willingly choose to join a conversation at a party, you might not find that the conversation is entirely relevant to you or very interesting. However, despite this, you might still be part of the conversation for a long period of time, even if a few people start a chat between themselves within the wider group chat (such as discussing a night out that only they are able to attend) which does not involve everyone. This is one of the biggest differences between conversations in the First Dimension and conversations in the Third Dimension. In First Dimension conversations, participants do not spend excessive amounts of time engaging in conversations that are past their prime because they fear the consequences of leaving. When a First Dimension conversation has reached a natural end, and a participant or participants have acted accordingly by removing themselves from it, assuming there has been no drama, others do not fret or frantically chase them to find out why they have left and try to draw them back in. Even in the Second Dimension, a phone call is ended with a goodbye and a handwritten letter with a closing statement. When participants leave a Third Dimension chat, if they are brave enough to, their decision might cause drama. The worst part is that leaving the group chat means entering unknown territory, something that does not happen when you end a conversation in the First Dimension.

Chapter 4

The Positives and Negatives of Group Chats

From the title, you would be forgiven for assuming that this book conveys a negative view of instant messengers and group chats, but that is not the intention. Instant messenger group chats play many roles in our lives that are both positive and negative, and in this book, I am exploring how there can be a more balanced relationship between people, their smartphones and the content contained within. In order to reach this balance, it is important to understand and acknowledge both the positive and negative ways that group chats on instant messengers can affect our lives, and that is what the chapter will discuss.

The Positive Sides of Instant Messenger Group Chats
We Want to Take Part in Group Chats
We are humans first and foremost and we naturally like and want to be involved in conversations with other

people, whatever that might look like. Even though many conversations have transferred to the digital realm, the positive aspects of being part of a digital conversation are not too different from the positive aspects being part of a conversation in the real world and the reasons for wanting to take part are the same.

There are four main things that entice us to converse with groups of other people in the first place. The first of these is the other people who are part of the conversation; our friends or family or anyone we would like to get to know better or learn from. We want to talk to them because we are social creatures and conversation enhances our bonds with others.

We could also gain something personal from conversing with others other than strengthening social bonds, which brings us nicely to reason number two. The second reason for wanting to be part of a group conversation is to be part of a discussion about an interesting topic of conversation. In the First Dimension this might usually happen organically at a party or informal gathering where there are many people who we could choose to converse with. People would allow themselves to be drawn into a conversation because they have overhead someone talking and what they have said sounds interesting, even if they do not know anyone else who is part of the conversation. In this instance the topic alone is enough to encourage us to be enthusiastic and engaged, whether it could be that a very interesting or amusing story is being told or because something intellectual is being discussed. If the topic is appealing to us, we can get something positive out of it mentally: a boost of serotonin and possibly a positive memory. There is also the chance that we could make new friends due to a shared interest. Even if we do not make new friends from this discussion, just taking part in it definitely adds enjoyment to the event at which the conversation has taken place, and if this person has someone or something in common, such as a friend or line of work, the anticipation that the same speakers might be at other events that we could attend in future is a personal bonus.

The third reason for wanting to be part of a group chat in the First Dimension is so that we do not have any fears of missing out, a term that is used enough in everyday life to be granted its own abbreviation – FOMO. FOMO has really come into its own as we have shared more and more titbits of information on social media, and as our access to news has increased from a daily newspaper and a few broadcasts a day on a given TV channel to twenty-four-seven news coverage across multiple dedicated channels, radio, apps, and the internet. Being constantly bombarded with endless information and insights into each other's lives might have amplified our FOMO because as humans we want to be part of social activities. Just look at the challenges that have gone viral around the world on platforms such as Instagram and TikTok – I am sure you would never have doused yourself in milk or eaten a tablespoon of cinnamon (please do not do this!) of your own accord. We do these crazy things not only because they are fun (or perceived to be fun) but also because we are humans and we want not only to belong, but to really feel part of something. Myers and Anderson sum it up best when they state that what that means regarding conversations is that they can be "exciting when joint efforts are recognised and celebrated, when relationships with new people are formed and when you can identify your contributions to making a small group endeavour successful" (Scott A. Myers, 2008). Things that could count as a 'group endeavour' could be small, such as being included in a joke with family, or larger, such as taking part in planning an activity like a hen party that everyone is looking forward to on a given weekend. Although they are referring specifically to smaller group conversations, what Myers and Anderson detail in this example can be applied to groups of all sizes, and even group conversations which take place via an instant messenger in the Third Dimension. Through sharing the same topics of interest, such as a silly anecdote about someone's day or information about the new James Bond film that is coming out soon, participants can become closer whether they are talking in-person, virtually or remotely.

The fourth reason for wanting to be part of a group conversation is because it could be a source of support. This is where the remote, private, and instant natures of the instant messaging app give it an advantage over conversations in the First Dimension. A study carried out by Queen Mary University in London looked at new mothers who use instant messengers and the results suggest that WhatsApp groups are a vital tool to help them navigate the role of being a mum for the first time after the birth of their first child. The study found that "the instant nature of the private WhatsApp groups, and the 'always on' character of the exchanges, can provide a round-the-clock support network in a way the NHS [British National Health Service] could not" (Lyons, 2020). The mums that were involved in the survey found that information from other mums was invaluable because it was consistent, accessible and free. This means that every mother could use it regardless of their economic status. Some services that a new mother might want to ordinarily access in order to assist her with being and becoming a parent could normally be available for a charge, and, due to the unpredictable nature of motherhood, it might not be available right when she might need it. Because the instant messenger is a remote tool that is always accessible, a mother or father can access it anywhere at any time.

Easy, Instant Communication

Another very obvious positive thing about a group chat on a messaging app is that it can make it very easy to communicate important information instantly and quickly. This is the very reason why this medium was developed in the first place and widely adopted. When used in our everyday lives, of which the instant messaging app has very much become an essential part, the ease of which we can communicate important information instantly and quickly via group chats is useful in such circumstances as when we have to find each other at an unfamiliar destination or when we need to let many people know that we are running late for an appointment. A work group chat was useful one morning when I was on the way to the office and, unbeknown to me, the building was closed due to a burst pipe in the area. A quick message in the group chat let my colleagues and I know this instantly, and I could promptly turn around and head back home to work from there instead.

Communicating Without Communicating

Another way in which instant messengers, and group chats in particular, have made it easier for us to communicate is through non-communication. Non-communication means that someone has communicated information to us indiscriminately and indirectly without specifically or intentionally telling us anything. For example, a chat participant can randomly tell the rest of the group about something that happened in their life such as getting engaged or buying a new car, and without seeking out this information or being told directly, we know about it now too. Through this type of non-communication, we can keep an eye on others and know a lot about their lives without intending to, or even when we no longer have any contact with them at all. Depending on the chat, this news might not be of interest, or very relevant, to everyone, however, everyone who is participating in the chat will now know about the news regardless. For some people, this ability to not communicate with others is seen as an asset, especially if they have friends and family who live far away from them. These people feel that friends and family can keep in touch with what is happening in their lives and vice versa with minimal effort. It might also be nice to meet friends in the knowledge that you do not have to go through the agony of announcing your recent divorce to them because they already know all about it. And who does not enjoy a bit of gossip?

Keeping In Contact and Building Bonds

It cannot be understated what a huge asset the remote nature of instant messaging apps is. Normally, if people do not see each other in person or see each other as much as they used to (which is very much the norm in Western-orientated societies after you reach your mid-twenties) due to moving away or leading busy lives, the relationships between these people will almost inevitably become weaker. Although this is never guaranteed, and I can definitely think of people who I can meet after years of little or no contact and know that we will continue to interact with each other as if we had never been apart, many relationships are said to decay with time if they are not sustained and maintained. For existing friendships, social media and instant messengers are said to reduce the rate at which relationships can decay if people are unable to see each other regularly or over a long period of time. This is because instant messaging apps allow people who might be apart for long periods or physically far away from each other to keep in contact easily, consistently, and more often. One researcher has even gone as far as to state that the messenger's role in preventing relationship decay is so important that it could be the main reason for the existence of social media in the first place:

"Social media may function mainly to prevent friendships decaying over time in the absence of opportunities for face-to-face contact. Given that people generally find interactions via digital media (including the phone as well as instant messaging and other text-based social media) less satisfying than face-to-face interactions, it may be that face-to-face meetings are required from time to time to prevent friendships, in particular, sliding down through the network layers and eventually slipping over the edge of the 150 layers into the category of acquaintances." (Dunbar, 2015.)

As well as preventing friendship decay, the group chat can provide a channel through which new bonds can be formed in the first place. One example of group chat participants bonding is illustrated nicely by a study which looked at some Israeli schoolchildren and their teachers who were using WhatsApp to aid their learning. They found that bonds between the students themselves, and bonds between the students and their teachers, were enhanced by being a part of a group chat on an instant messaging app.

"One of the groups that I started to teach started the year with students who did not have anything in common and many social conflicts. Establishing a WhatsApp group and encouraging the group to take part in it, contributed to the positive atmosphere in that class." T8 [teacher number 8] continued, "The students need it; the group gave them a sense of belonging. They want to be part of the group."

T7 [teacher number 7] added, "A student that left the class, asked to stay part of the group, and even participated in the conversation from time to time. He said that he still wants to be part of the group although he does not study with them anymore." It seems that belonging to a WhatsApp group reinforced the student's connection to the class (Dan Bouhnik, 2014).

This study shows that social bonds can be enhanced if the digital conversation that happens between people is used to supplement meetings held in the First Dimension. It also further illustrates that one very positive aspect of group chats on instant messengers is that they can be an important source of support. Just like the new mums mentioned above, the students in the study had a way to reach out for help with their studies. In the same vein, the participants in the hen do chat will be able to get to know each other before meeting, at least to some extent. This could make things a bit easier for all involved by providing conversation starters as each participant learns about the other participants in the group. The chat can also make it easier to not only to form, but to access social bonds that might already exist (to an extent) but might feel faint or out of reach. A chat that is made up of old childhood schoolfriends can give participants a channel that enables them to reach out to people who they might otherwise not ordinarily speak to. If you want to go for a drink, and you are not sure who to ask to go out with you (or you are generally a bit shy to approach people) you can message a group chat of people who live locally and see who responds. The one who responds to your message might not even be the person who you expected would respond.

Group chats are also fun, at least for a period of their existence, which explains their continued popularity. It is great to share jokes, stories and to have that continuous connection with people that you like, it is also an easy thing to do if you are bored. I, for one, have definitely sent out some very generic "how are you?" messages during moments of my life that have been a bit dull – and the responses that I have received have helped. The randomness is part of the joy – in a group chat, with other participants, you are never quite sure where the conversation will take you.

The Negatives of Group Chats

"Online we discuss things only through text. I think we should not be surprised that we're having so much difficulty in finding the right way to discuss and co-operate online." (Vince, 2018.)

Obliged to Join, Obliged to Stay

The first thing to mention when talking about the negative aspects of group chats on instant messengers is that it could very well be the case that you did not agree to be part of that group chat in the first place. Ordinarily, people can add participants at will, and this non-agreement can cancel out the benefits of being part of a group chat and even make you reluctant to join any group chats in the future at all. You might even have been voluntold – whereby you were told that you were being added but did not have any space to voice an objection. You were added to the group chat even though you would have preferred not to take part and that the person who added you had not added you in the first place. Now you are taking part in the chat, you will not be exiting it any time soon, and it could last a while.

Group chats can continue even when there is nothing to talk about (and not in the romantic sense). One of linguist David Crystal's golden rules of conversation is that for a conversation to continue, "there has to be a topic that is capable of continued treatment" (Crystal, 2020). Often, group chats in the Third Dimension break this rule. Before instant messaging apps came to smartphones, never before in history has a conversation gone on so long whilst participants have simultaneously been (or felt) obliged to remain part of it, because even if there is no longer a topic that everyone involved in the group chat can talk about together, the unwritten and assumed rules surrounding the group chat mean that participants are unlikely to leave the chat when they otherwise normally would. Myers and Anderson note that frustrations might arise here due to "the lack of co-operation that may exist among members [e.g. if one person is talked over and not allowed to join in the conversation], the possibility of the emergence of conflict and the clash of personalities among group members" (Scott A. Myers, 2008). For these reasons and more, participants in a conversation might not want to be part of that conversation any longer, yet in the Third Dimension the group chat can continue even if it does not involve you or is irrelevant to you. Once you are in the chat, you are very likely stuck in the chat. The chat might not even be continuous, but despite that, you feel like you cannot get away. This is something which can be frustrating in itself. The longevity of group chats means that they can die down temporarily. Between those periods of conversation there can be a long period of silence, and then, just as you think a chat is dead, someone can revive it.

We Cannot See Each Other

I refer back to the lack of a common topic that Crystal mentions and feel that it is worth noting that this, as well as Myers' lack of co-operation, might not necessarily be intentional. It has been mentioned already, but we cannot ignore that in a group chat the usual markers such as body language, tone of voice, facial expressions and eye contact that would guide and keep a conversation under control in the real world are absent. Without such essential cues – the very things that make us human – there is a greater margin for misjudgement. This absence leaves the chat vulnerable to become boring or emotional, or dominated by one person. And there might never have been a common topic of conversation because no one else might have liked the main topic of conversation in the first place – they just never said so.

The lack of body language and vocals means that participants are more likely not to know when to take a step back, or when to take their chat away from the group chat, unless another participant explicitly tells them so. This means that participants are more likely to behave in ways which can be perceived as daunting, awkward, or annoying. It is common for a couple of participants, or a few participants, to have a conversation amongst themselves that excludes most of the group. Because no one can physically see each other, each participant will often just respond to the text that appears on the screen and they can soon become engrossed in a conversation that does not involve everyone, even though they might not be fully aware that they are leaving people out. This absence makes it unclear in a group chat on an instant messenger where boundaries lie, and the other chat participants may not know if or when to intervene and inform the speakers that the conversation no longer includes them. Any passive chat participants, that is people who might be observing the conversation but not contributing, will not be able to see the reactions of the other participants in the chat and as a result they will also be unsure if the others agree with their opinion of what is said in the chat and if they will be backed up if they do intervene. The action of speaking up is always a risky one anyway, regardless of where a conversation takes place, and therefore the easiest thing to do in this situation is to say nothing and remain silent.

Alter Egos

Friends can behave differently on social media and in group chats to how they would behave in real life. You might dislike something about how a person is in the group chat, even if you adore them normally. This could cause friction, unspoken resentment, or for you to distance yourself from that friend. In a similar vein, when using the group chat to arrange exciting events like a hen do or your children's school fete, you might find yourself disliking the other participants due to the way that they present themselves in the group chat. This can be due to the fact that First Dimension conversational cues are missing, but also because behind the façade of a digital screen people can create a persona allowing other chat participants to get to know a very carefully (or perhaps not so carefully) constructed personality – see the example of Amy in Chapter 3. This dislike can lead to a chat participant feeling uncomfortable about attending an event if they worry that they will have to spend time with people that they have a negative impression of. It is possible that participants might feel inadequate compared to other people in the chat, such as in this example of Rebecca Preedy, a fresher who blogged for the University of Warwick when she was a student there. Rebecca felt uncomfortable when joining a WhatsApp group chat before starting her degree in Ancient History and Classical Archaeology. Although she was initially excited about starting university and the subject that she was studying, her unease grew due to the fact that everyone else in the group appeared to be more experienced and knowledgeable than her about the subject that they were all about to study. In her own words:

"Before I had even arrived at Warwick and taken my first class, I was seeing messages from people who had been studying classics for years, from a variety of backgrounds, all discussing their experiences, grades, and other expected chit-chat from recent A-level graduates. Until that moment, Classics and Ancient History had been a hobby for me, something that I had not studied academically and that none of my peers at school shared with me. It was a terrifying moment to be surrounded by so many people who had already taken classes and exams in the subject, and there was a moment of self-doubt for me." (Preedy, 2020.)

Who Is Your Friend?

The accessible nature of social media has given us a larger collection of friends than we have evolved to cope with. According to a 2015 study from the University of Oxford, based on the historic sizes of societies, we will put all of our effort into managing to keep in contact with no more than 150 people overall, a number which accounts for friends, family, colleagues, people in industry, such as shopkeepers and bus drivers, and so on. This is the average maximum amount of people that any one person is said to be able to manage and we do not dedicate our time and resources to all 150 people equally but dole it out accordingly with most of our energy dedicated to around fifteen friends. This more manageable number of fifteen friends frequently falls very short of the number of Facebook friends which any one person can have. These can run into the hundreds. In a social media context, 'friend' is a term which has evolved to suggest a more distant connection, and with this has come the term 'Facebook friend'. Facebook friends are people we are linked to via the social networking platform but may only ever have met once, no matter how brief the encounter. Before social media, it was unusual to keep any kind of contact with people whom we barely knew. Now, a lot of our energy is dedicated to keeping up with hundreds of lives on a daily basis, and that is in addition to the people and activities that we have to dedicate energy to in the real world. Facebook friends have made it acceptable to keep in touch with people we barely know in group chats too. As these platforms have evolved, sites such as Facebook, LinkedIn and Instagram even add to this burden by displaying updates from accounts that you do not even choose to follow. All of this can be tiring, yet even so it has become too culturally acceptable to participate in group chats consisting of people that you hardly or do not know. Whereas once you might politely have exchanged phone numbers safe in the knowledge that you probably will never ring that person, now they are part of yet another group chat that you are part of whether you like it or not – and they can contact you at will around the clock.

To add to this, the group chat has become another avenue through which we can stalk others. This is something which we touched on in the introduction. Stalking in the digital sense can be both passive (e.g. we happen to find out information about people because they typed it into the group chat) and active (e.g. we deliberately scrolled through a person's Facebook history to find out information about them). Knowing so much about others all of the time, and knowing that they know about you, can be stressful and exhausting especially when it concerns individuals that you would either rather not be connected to, or individuals that you would actually like to see in the real world but are unable to do so. Can you ever think of a time where you have gone down a black hole just browsing different social profiles belonging to people you would hardly spare a thought for the in the First Dimension? By engaging in such actions we can unwittingly be stretching ourselves beyond our friendship limit. Stalking has led to ghosting, a term that describes when people break contact with people who they know well and may have been extremely close to, and then proceed to stalk them on social media. It can be very upsetting for people to be ghosted by someone who used to be a good friend because the real feelings for them are still there.

The Phone is Now Your Friend

Our use of social media has changed our idea of what a friend is and even the smartphone itself has been described as a 'companion', transcending the line between man and machine as we attach our emotions to it. This was noted by Münch et al. when studying factors that influenced how willing people were to take part in a digital detox:

"Users' constant interaction with the phone has been shown to result in some kind of relationship between owner and device which was referred to as a 'digital compan-ionship'. They even compared this relationship with characteristics of a human relationship leading to the idea that the smartphone is more than just a technical device but rather a digital companion." (Catharina Münch, 2020.)

The fact that we love inanimate objects is nothing new – there is a reason why young children have teddies and dolls, and my main houseplants have names. In studies conducted on human beings and how we relate to objects that are not alive, MRI scans show that areas of the brain light up when an inanimate object is given affection and when it is subjected to suffering. They are similar to the areas which light up when people witness other humans being given affection or suffering. However, the adoration that we have for our smartphones is quite different to simply loving the device as we might love a favourite teddy bear. Here we are enamoured with the contents of the device and the rewarding experiences that it can give us in a digital realm. A 2021 study from a team at University College London (UCL) further illustrated just how important smartphones have become in people's lives around the world. The study observed smartphone use in nine quite different countries, including Ireland, Cameroon, Brazil and Japan and the results suggested that smartphones are as important to human beings today as having a home, and instant messaging services, predominantly WhatsApp, WeChat (a Chinese messaging app) and LINE (a Japanese messaging app) are described as 'the heart of the smartphone' (Miller, 2021).

Too Much in One Place

When you are part of a group chat, the group chat will very likely become the medium through which that particular group will share all of their information. If you rely on the chat for important information, you could spend a lot of time scrolling through the chat history in order to try and find it. If you are the person who has the patience to spend a lot of time scrolling, or the one who usually organises events, you are also likely the person who people will repeatedly ask for information because they do not have the patience or the common sense to spend a lot of time scrolling back through the chat for information that was previously provided to them, despite the fact that you have given them your home address or directions to the pub ten times. This is tiring, even more so because the chat does not ever switch off and the content within it continues to grow. I refer back to the 2015 study from the University of Oxford that suggests that both the size of our neocortex and the time we have available to us in our daily lives limit how much energy we can invest in friendships. We do not have the physical or mental capacity to keep up with conversations from so many people, and we do not want chat participants who we might be conversing with through circumstance to take up our friend allowance. Even talking constantly to the people who we do know can be exhausting, as this example from Mumsnet user Lizzie523 demonstrates:

"When lockdown started we made a Facebook group for all of us and have done video chats ever since. Now, the one-to-one friendships have dissolved and we only ever talk on this group chat now. It's always 'when are you all free to talk??' and to be honest I've had enough of it for now. I just want to go back to our 1 to 1 friendships with occasional overlap/group chats." (Lizzie523, 2020.)

Lizzie523 said that she felt closer to some of the friends in the group chat than others, and these were not all people who she would have normally interacted with every day anyway. This situation made her feel exasperated with the group chat and it is easy to see why she preferred to interact with each of the friends individually as she did before. By focusing only on group chats, you could unintentionally drift from your friends like Lizzie523, who ended up feeling like she had drifted from the group of friends she had cherished for years. Adding to this, if you tell your friends all of your news and gossip before you meet them, when you do meet up, is there anything left to talk about?

Virtual group chats held on instant messaging apps can be enjoyable and serve a purpose. If they did not there would be no reason to take part in them in the first place. However, there are also downsides to being part of a conversation that never ends, is almost always constantly nearby and rarely out of mind. Instant messaging group chats, both in the first and third dimensions, can be both positive and negative, and the positive aspects are great enough to contribute to the fact that it is very difficult for participants to leave.

Chapter 5

Grouping Chats

In the previous chapters we have discussed how conversations work within the different dimensions in which they take place. We looked at the positives and negatives of talking to people in a group, and why we might want to take part in a conversation or not. Now in this chapter, we will look at the different types of group chats that exist on instant messengers in the Third Dimension and discover that not all group chats are created equal, despite having similar functions and overlaps.

Hoßfeld et al. say that there are three categories of group chat: Unique Event Groups (e.g. a birthday party), Repetitive Event Groups (e.g. a regular social gathering) and No Event Groups (e.g. a group of family members). (Tobias Hoßfeld, 2015.) Trying to group chats, especially under three categories as broad as these, it could be argued, is difficult because instant messaging group chats vary as much as any conversation would in the First Dimension. There are groups for families, siblings, old friends, new friends, neighbours and entire neighbourhoods, parents of children who attend the same school, playdates, party guests, sports clubs, work colleagues and groups that might be a combination of these. Each of these has their similarities and differences, they overlap and the purposes of each chat change and evolve over time, as do the people taking part in them. The biggest difference, according to Hoßfeld's study, is time. It concludes that any chats discussing a unique event (such as a party) last around six months, whereas other types of chats can continue for years.

To complement each chat there could be one or a few sub-chats in which some of the same participants from the parent chat (meaning the main chat) hold a conversation that the parent group is not privy to. The (somewhat more extreme) example given below of CharDee's many group chats illustrates nicely how this works:

"DH's family on the other hand is something else. He has a sister and BiL [Brother in Law] as well as another brother, his wife and their children who live down south. With them we have the following group chats:

» All the family (PILs [parents-in-law], SIL [sister-in-law] and her DH [daughter's husband], BIL [brother-in-law] and DW [daughter's wife], me and DH)
» Local family (all of the above apart from BIL and DW)
» Updates on Coronavirus (local family)
» Updates on DS (about our son which is just for local family)
» Sibling chat with SIL, her DH and me
» Just DH and SIL
» Updates on DN (about SIL's son which is for all family)
» Shopping (local family)

» Food (local family)
» Updates for all the children (shared with all family)."
(CharDee, 2020.)

There is no denying that to categorise every group chat would be an encyclopaedia unto itself. So where to begin? In this this chapter we will look at some of the more common types of group chat which you will probably be familiar with: the family chat, the friendship group chat and the work group chat and these will be used to demonstrate many of the issues with group chats overall and give examples of how they can work in practise.

The Family Chat

A family chat group is an instant messaging group chat that is made up of members of a family. There are lots of stereotypes of older people and technology, and yes, it did take my father a good few years to realise that, yes, he does have WhatsApp on his phone (my sister downloaded it for him) and that, at the time of finally discovering how it works, he already had a message from each of us (each of us being the sister and I). We had a good laugh about that. Mum worked it out too and a WhatsApp group was formed. Time has passed since that miraculous day and we are still in the group, now playing Wordle every day, plus my aunt has joined us now since she has finally upgraded to a smartphone. Unlike family chats on a smartphone, family chats in the First Dimension used to signify that there was something serious to discuss, unlike family gatherings which usually celebrate a special occasion (at least, they did in my family). The family chat in the Third

Dimension is not held for any particular reason other than to have a chat with your family. It can be a mixture of both chat and gathering, and everything in between.

Parents in Your Pocket

There is a reason why as people become teenagers they spend less and less time with their parents before eventually fleeing the nest, and it is not so that you can have your parents in your pocket. "By pushing away from adults and hanging out more with peers during our adolescence, we can find new ways of dealing with the world and create new strategies for living." (Siegel, 2014.) And, as offspring make that transition from child to adult, teenagers experiment with everything from what they like and how they look to where boundaries are and which sort of person they may settle down with one day. It is essential to distance yourself from your family in order to undertake this and to become your own person. Once this transition is complete, grown-up family members then settle into the routine of their own adult lives and eventually the retirement years. So the cycle continues. The older members of the family will always be part of your life and very important to you, but is it healthy to be messaging your parents every day, and to be available to them round the clock when, as Hassler puts it quite simply:

"In order to fully mature and develop a sense of self, one needs to make decisions on his or her own. Having Mom on speed dial at the ready to answer any question from what to wear to how to deal with a challenge at work prolongs the adolescence period of one's life." (Hassler, 2008.)

Social media, through providing a shared, accessible platform full of copycat behaviour, has prolonged

73

adolescence, and arguably pulled some older adults back into adolescence. This is another behaviour which has filtered into the realm of the Third Dimension and the instant messenger group chat. In the past, children and adults had their place in an established hierarchy of age, status and experience, even when coming together to engage in the same activities. By prolonging adolescence, this hierarchy has been disrupted. This disruption is reflected more generally across social media with terms such as 'kidult' and 'adulting' entering the mainstream. People are reluctant to grow up. On social media it is also common to see parents referring to their children of all ages as their #bestie or #bestfriend as well as #minime. The use of such terms suggests that adolescence has not just been prolonged, but the boundary between parent and friend has also been blurred. It is reasonable to suspect that this blurred boundary has occurred as a result of children and their parents sharing the same technological platforms that allow them to present themselves in the same ways, because people inherently copy what others are doing. When you are seeing so many people engaging in the same mannerisms and activities every single day, it would be natural to become more familiar with them and to engage with them without giving too much thought as to what might be age-appropriate. We do not just see this every day; we are bombarded with such imagery!

Jumping In

Alongside blurred boundaries, there is also the worry that the constant contact that parents and children have on social media has led to parents not only seeing their children more as buddies than offspring, but also having a much greater insight into their lives. Prior to social media, parents would not know in photographic detail what their children (of all ages) get up to with their friends, but we are talking about something beyond the old folks knowing too much about that messy Saturday night at 'Spoons. Parents do not only know too much about their children's lives, but there are fears that they are doing too much for their children and stepping in to help them too often. This has become such a big issue that it has even become a concern for schools. School group chats on WhatsApp and Facebook messenger have become popular in recent years, but as well as children forming groups with other children, parents have formed groups with other parents in the same year group so that they can keep tabs on everything from inset days and homework assignments to remembering PE kits and even intervening when children have issues with their friends. Some schools, such as Wimbledon High School in West London, have told parents not to engage in such groups, because, in the case of high school pupils in particular, children need to be encouraged to look after their own affairs, make their own mistakes and develop their own organisational skills (Bennett, 2020) in order to, as Hassler (above) puts it, "fully mature and develop a sense of self". These groups can also be huge, quickly resulting in a message overload. A friend showed me a school group chat that she was in – her WhatsApp display informed us that she had seven hundred unread messages. The school kids also decided to form a WhatsApp group, with six hundred messages displaying on her child's phone. Unsurprisingly, such high numbers meant that neither mother nor child were reading any of those messages, and, kids being kids, child was tired of the pranksters in the group constantly calling every single member at the same time. They did not bother to answer those phone calls either.

Acting Out

Parent/child relationship aside, in families each family member plays a role. Relationship expert Charlie Bloom explains why the role that each family member has becomes an important part of our identity:

"Family roles that are played out in most families become so solidly reinforced in childhood that they are integrated into our identity and cemented into our sense of who we are. Consequently, they not only get played out in our adult relationships, but we develop a strong attachment to embodying them." (Charlie Bloom, 2017.)

Most family members are not even aware of their family role, and almost all members of a family may perceive the role that each family member has very differently to each other. However, within the confines of the never-ending family group chat, each of the family roles may become obvious to others as each member acts out their role in the family unit. This can be annoying or stressful, especially if you can see that you play a certain role but cannot work out how to deviate from it. Parents can share umpteen numbers of bad jokes, avoid certain topics that they might avoid in the real world or tell grown-up children off for things that they are too old to be told off for. You may find that the WhatsApp group chat brings out your competitive side as sibling after sibling shows off their amazing achievements to your parents, just like when you were children. Your brother or sister might be very talented, clever and successful. They might be a straight-A student, undertake a prestigious internship and effortlessly work their way up in a company whilst posting videos of their amazing baking creations on YouTube. They might constantly promote these achievements in the family group chat (it is not so farfetched to imagine that some may do this daily) and each announcement might be met with adoring emojis and compliments that are over the top. You are probably proud of them, as well as perhaps a little envious, and it will not be long before you feel the need to compete as the stressful feelings build up. It is not just another family member's content that is exhausting, but the volume of images shared, the repetitive nature of the conversation and the outpouring of emotion that can at times be too much. In the First Dimension you would hear about some of these achievements, but not every day. On Facebook you can choose what to look at; in a family group chat, you also do not have any choice over what you see or hear – the entire feed of messages will be placed in front of you like courses at a posh restaurant.

Stuck With You

Then there may be families who do not like each other very much, or at the very least would prefer to keep a distance from each other, but, as the earlier example of CharDee's many WhatsApp groups demonstrates, many family members are often obliged to be part of the family group chat in order to keep the peace for the benefit of their other half, another family member who they are close to or even just to ensure order within the entire family, even if they do not particularly want to engage with other family members on such a frequent basis. There is nothing to stop someone in a family group chat from extending the invitation to the WhatsApp group chat to other family members who you might know or like to varying degrees. CharDee said that she had always seen her sister-in-law as controlling. The two had had an argument and given that there was pressure to take part in so many group chats on a frequent basis, on top of whatever issues there may have been in the First Dimension, this is unsurprising. Other family members were privy to this outburst, and because they witnessed it, it became inevitable that some of these other family members would also eventually become involved in the argument (CharDee, 2020). More members in a group chat can equal more irritation, especially if you have to communicate with someone you do not get along with on a frequent basis. There is no denying that the obligation for CharDee to take part in so many group chats involving just one family was a big ask in itself.

At the other end of the spectrum, talking more frequently in a group chat can mean that you might talk to your family a lot more than you used to, and that in turn can bring people closer together (if you like them, that is). Before talking to my own family in a group chat, I did not really have any idea what my sister was up to wherever she was living, and we did not communicate anywhere near as frequently.

The family group chat can be useful for announcements. Because instant messengers are remote tools, users can use the group chat to mention the new baby on the way or that the dog has died without having to tell everyone individually. The people in the chat will know about these important life events before you are able to meet them, and likewise, armed with this knowledge they can prepare themselves for when they do see you next. This can cut out a lot of the additional stress and awkward moments that people would have experienced in the First Dimension prior to instant messaging or social media because previously you had to tell a lot of different individuals or groups of people important news individually and deal with their reactions each in turn as they absorbed the news right before you. Gone is the daunting prospect of facing a large announcement in front of people where you have to think about every aspect of delivering that news. However, although I can tell people my major news before meeting them, it does not mean that I will talk about something new when I meet the people I have told in-person and this means that First Dimension conversations, with some people at least, might become limited.

Another flip side of using instant messengers to share announcements is that, due to the nature of the group chat being boundless and timeless, there may be too many announcements. This can be annoying, as demonstrated by a Mumsnet user's comment below:

"My SIL [sister-in-law], who has a history of posting school reports and the like on Facebook, has now started to post test scores and frequent achievement updates for my nephew. I do like to hear about them, but it does not do my head any good to hear daily how marvellous he is. My MIL [mother-in-law] will want to hear, and I'd expect her to want to, but I do not need that level of detail, particularly when I'm having a bad day with one of mine. When I share stuff, I do it by email or individual WhatsApp. Add to that the fact that it is always about my nephew, never my niece, despite both being on the group and I just cannot bear it." (ilovearticroll, 2019.)

Problem Solving

As well as being used to announce good things, some people take solace in the group chat as a means to talk through problems which might be easier to discuss without the heated emotions that would inevitably be present in the First Dimension. Turkle talks about this and calls it the Goldilocks Effect in her book Reclaiming Conversation: The Power of Talk in a Digital Age, and how behind a cover such as an instant messenger, people are free to construct and edit their words and ultimately their own presentation of themselves:

"Some refer to this practice as 'fighting by text'. They tell me [Turkle] that electronic talk 'keeps the peace' because with this regime, there are no out-of-control confrontations. Tempers never flare. One mother argues that when family members do not fear outbursts, they are more likely to express their feelings." (Turkle, 2015.)

In the same way that Amy who we met in Chapter 3 felt more comfortable making conversation with boys behind the anonymous identity of the instant messenger, in the Third Dimension there might still be bad tempers and ill feelings between family members, however, they might not be so evident from the textual conversation and in turn, the conversation will not be as intimidating to other participants.

Friendship Group Chats

One important reason for instant messengers becoming so popular is because they allow people to connect with friends and maintain friendships, and that is certainly how instant messaging started for me. Long before I had a smartphone, everyone in my class at high school was adding each other to the brand-new MSN Messenger which we used on desktop computers. Back in the day, when teenage lives were much more secretive and boundaries were not so blurred, MySpace was where you would connect with friends, not parents. Your parents were getting excited about Friends Reunited, a site that allowed them to connect with former schoolfriends their own age. The Facebook friend came into existence as the definition of friend took on a whole new meaning – the person who added you was not always your friend in the First Dimension.

Social media set the precedence for loosely defining friends, and therefore the friendship group chat can be defined as a group chat that is made up of friends, acquaintances or friends and acquaintances. It might also include a family member or two, but generally the family members present would be the minority (otherwise it would be a family chat, not a friendship group chat) – perhaps a few siblings or cousins would be in the same group chat with several other friends. This group chat does not have a defined purpose. It could be said that the friendship group chat is the one that most accurately reflects the personalities of the people in the group, due to the fact that there is no hierarchy, and the participants present are likely to be of a similar age. This is the type of WhatsApp group that, especially if you know everyone, can be a lot of fun because the subject matter is likely to be more causal with fewer formalities. I have been in some which almost entirely consist of sharing jokey GIFs and memes, some come with the odd request to meet up for a drink once in a while and others with very close mates that consist of a much deeper conversation, be it silly or sensible.

Keep In Touch

Friendship group chats can be a great way to catch-up with friends you have not seen for a while. They can also provide a way to reboot a relationship with someone who you otherwise might not have contact with. Almost all of my communication in friendship groups on WhatsApp is conducted via text messages, and I rarely speak on the telephone to anyone who I do not pay a direct debit to. Most of my friends live in different countries, so being able to communicate so often and so easily with them is a huge blessing, even if it is mostly by text. It is very telling that there are friends who I can communicate with, mostly via instant messages (with photos, emojis and funny videos thrown in), for years, however frequently or infrequently, and when we do meet in-person our friendship continues as it always has, regardless of the physical distance between us or the lack of real-world human contact. It is debatable how relevant this is to the fact that we have communicated via WhatsApp or whether our friendship is strong enough regardless of the fact that we use instant messengers, but it cannot be denied that instant messaging services can be a vital link to keep communication open when people change addresses and phone numbers. Having that line of communication could make the difference between a friend visiting London and letting me know, and a friend visiting London and not telling me that they are coming. One thing is for sure, the friends that I have the closest bonds with will always let me know when they are nearby.

Going Quiet

On the other side of the coin, there are other WhatsApp groups consisting of friends who do not live as far away from each other, where people are active and chatty. However, when a suggestion is made to meet up in-person, people either go quiet or frequently decline. The dynamics between the participants in these groups can be quite complex. Some of the participants living locally might be closer to some participants than others, and unless you have a good relationship with individuals in the group, leaving the group means that you will lose everyone in the group. As a result, you might be left out of social events altogether. There is also the double whammy when losing contact with people who live nearby, because even if you do not meet them very often, these are the people it would be useful to contact if you need any help with anything in the real world such as moving house or childminding. This can make it difficult to just exit a group even when participants are continually uninterested. However close you may feel to someone, rejection is hurtful and there are studies that suggest that being excluded from a group chat can be just as hurtful as being excluded from groups in the real world, if not more so, because the chat on your phone is a constant reminder of that exclusion:

"One thing that platforms like group chats facilitate is a more public, more apparent and more interactive ability to leave out folks," says Rebecca Hayes, an assistant professor of communication at Illinois State University, who studies social media interactions. "Yes, it has always hurt to realise you're no longer a member of a certain friend group, or that people you introduced now prefer each other's company to yours. But omnipresent digital conversations," Hayes says, "take processes that have existed since the beginning of time and amplify them in a way that might have a more enduring psychological impact."

So if a particular friendship group chat causes us grief, why do we remain in it? Sarah Buglass, a lecturer in social and cyber psychology at Nottingham Trent University (O'Kane, 2017), suggests that the reason we stay in WhatsApp groups, even if participants feel awkward, overwhelmed, or uncomfortable, may be due to feeling the fear of missing out, or FOMO:

"For some leaving a WhatsApp group is akin to saying, 'I do not want to be involved' – a message that may be far from the truth. Therefore, for some, lurking in the background allows them to maintain a social link to the group – not only to maintain a sense of belonging but also to indicate to the others that they are interested in being part of the group." (Gander, 2017.)

One group chat on my phone consists of unfamiliar names of people I have never met (along with people I know) and those people have not responded to anything since the very early days of the group which has been active for a good few years. As I do not know them, and I have never become acquainted with them, their silence is not something that affects me, but I cannot help wondering if they are even still active on that instant messenger and why they have not removed themselves from the group chat in question. These ghost participants might well be feeling FOMO, but they could also be monitoring the discussions for any mention of themselves (there have not been any) or any potential future social get-togethers. They could also be safeguarding themselves from any potentially negative social repercussions (Gander, 2017).

When You Do Not Get Along
It is possible that you might end up in a group with some people who you do not get on so well with, because your friends, the chat hosts, will not always remember exactly who you got along with and who you did not or a well-meaning friend might add you to a group made up of their friends who you do not know. But a group chat can really turn sour if you happen to fall out with someone else who is in the chat, or if others in the chat fall out with each other. It can be a shock when two people who previously got along are no longer friends. This is illustrated nicely in the below example from O'Kane, who talks about a situation that happened after his mutual friends Blair and Nelle broke up:

"In October, two of my good friends broke up... as a few of us sat around over drinks, my pal Tom quietly did the unthinkable. He kicked Nelle out of our 20-member Facebook Messenger chat. The room went silent. One friend lifted his phone up and pointed the screen at Tom, a gasp. "I'm just trying to be a friend to Blair," Tom said. For him, this meant cutting Nelle off from the place where we've made plans for three years – where it was always possible to find someone willing to meet up for beers, brunch or both. The breakup was already a shock. This was excommunication." (O'Kane, 2017.)

Whether Tom blamed Nelle for the breakup, or whether he happened to be closer to Blair, we cannot judge his actions. This scenario above may or may not be familiar, but it clearly conveys the awkwardness of a situation when people are no longer friends and that this can be even worse if someone in the friendship group chat decides to take sides. Naturally, the other participants will want to know what has happened, however intimate the details might be. They might ask other participants in the chat for these details, or they might continue in the chat and ignore the issue of the person who has left. Like O'Kane, chat participants may also feel guilty for siding with one person or the other.

TMI

Another problem, when participants in any given friendship group chat feel more comfortable with each other, is the tendency to overshare. This comes as no surprise because social media platforms actively encourage their users to share everything and anything about themselves. It makes them more interesting and they get more members and engagement. In conversations that happen in the First Dimension, oversharing would be more likely to occur within groups of friends, people who you would normally be more relaxed with anyway, than in groups with people you do not know as well or in groups involving participants you might normally be a bit more reserved or politer around, such as teachers or older family members. This would likely also be the case within friendship group chats that take place in the Third Dimension. A couple of people I knew who were in one group chat that I was in took a very expensive holiday to their dream destination. As happy as the other participants in the group were for them, for months and months this was all that they talked about. Photos were shared, and more photos and then a video compilation of their holiday – and another, the edited version. As lockdown started, they took part in activities with other friends, and told us all about them in our group chat. You have guessed it – everything referenced their holiday. After a point I did not respond for a while, not only because I was tired of the subject, but because when a conversation in which one subject is repeated past exhaustion, and especially when that subject is a subject that other people cannot relate to, there is only so much that can be said in response to that subject.

Another cause of awkwardness in group chats are those overly emotional 'thank yous' from one participant to another participant because Participant A has received an amazing birthday present ("Is it your birthday?") or a generous contribution to their skydiving charity fundraiser ("I did not know you were doing a charity skydive?"). When I have someone to thank, I personally message whoever has made a kind gesture in a separate chat and let them know how much I appreciate their action outside of the friendship group, because I would never want any of my friends to be surprised that they missed an event or for them to feel like they have been outdone because someone else's gesture was bigger or more expensive than their own. I would also never want anyone to feel obliged to contribute to anything that I was doing. There is no harm in asking for donations or contributions to an event. There is also no invalid reason for not wanting to take part in something or to contribute to something. I appreciate every gesture equally, no matter how big or small.

As much as you might adore each and every one of your friends and you are happy that they want you to be part of their friendship group chat, the sheer number of WhatsApp groups that exist on anyone's phone at any one time can be a headache, and it would be nice to have the option to end a conversation when it is not warranted. If any app developers are reading this, it would be great if there was a function to temporarily leave a group and then return if you felt like it, in the same way that you would enter and leave a conversation in the First Dimension. As good as group chats are, some things are just better said when you actually meet up with your friends and nothing can replace that.

The Work WhatsApp Group

"My phone has pinged this morning and I have found out I have been added to a WhatsApp group for work.

I'm not entirely happy about this.

1. it's my personal mobile
2. They have put my number into the group for all to see. Without my permission. Is it a breach of personal data?
3. We are all entitled to downtime away from work and Imo [in my opinion] this just encroaches into my work life balance too much.

Obviously I do not want to make trouble for myself but how should I approach the subject with my bosses?" (Nodiggidy123, 2017)

Work group chats consist of you and your colleagues, whether that means you and your immediate team or a group of colleagues who are more widespread in the office. It might surprise you to know that WhatsApp prohibits the use of the app for work purposes in its terms and conditions. Despite the fact that many businesses use it, most workers are unaware of this clause. This is interesting because instant messengers were originally created for business purposes. This lack of awareness in itself demonstrates what a normal presence instant messaging services are in our everyday lives. In 2020, a study by Guild found that 41% of 1,261 workers surveyed in the UK use WhatsApp for work purposes and this is very likely the tip of the iceberg (Guild, 2020). This number looks set to increase as among younger members of staff (defined as being aged forty-five and under) the rate at which workers used WhatApp for business purposes increased to just over half (53%). Instant messaging services can be a very useful tool for businesses to communicate their needs quickly and efficiently, share documents and information and to find each other at events such as conferences. Groups of colleagues also use them for fun or banter.

Invading Your Home Life

Some work WhatsApp groups are contained on business phones, which, if you do not use your business phone as your private phone, might not so bad because you only see the messages when you are on duty – at least in theory. If the WhatsApp group is on your private phone, you could find that work matters start to infiltrate your private life when you are off-duty, thus upsetting the essential work-life balance that is needed for every employee's well-being. The inability to switch off from work has received a lot of attention during the Covid-19 pandemic with members of staff primarily (if not entirely) working from home, but it was considered a problem before 2020, prompting countries such as France to pass laws banning staff from contacting employees outside of their working hours. A finishing time should be a finishing time, days off are days off and members of staff should not be chased via WhatsApp off the clock.

Fine Lines

There was always a fine line between being friends and being colleagues, and still is, even if you get along with your colleagues extremely well. Although we are only human, and do make friends in the workplace, working relationships should ideally be kept more disciplined and professional for the duration of your employment in order to avoid any external or personal issues affecting the company or yourself as an employee. For this reason, work group chats are a liability because, as well as being used for business purposes, they are also used for office banter. Due to the fact that vital elements, such as visible body language, which control conversations in the real world are missing from such conversations, that boundary between friend and colleague is liable to be blurred even further. This could encourage employees to lower their guard and post items in a chat that might not be appropriate in the workplace. Those employees could therefore unintentionally end up in trouble, either posting something that is inoffensive but does not comply with the company's ethos or rules (such as political memes in a Civil Service chat) or posting something that causes offence or discomfort among other employees (such as something that mocks religion). One famous workplace dispute was in 2020 when former Prime Minister Boris Johnson's former adviser Dominic Cummings publicised some inappropriate exchanges between himself and Johnson. In these instant messaging exchanges, the Prime Minister allegedly insulted and criticised Matt Hancock, who was health secretary at the time. Using WhatsApp in this manner could have unforeseen legal consequences, especially as employees have the ability to message each other discreetly under the radar of the business. Law firm Simpson Millar states that this can cause problems if employees complain or raise a grievance about bullying, harassment, or degrading treatment on WhatsApp. The firm states that some of the questions raised from such conduct are:

"Do they [a company] commence disciplinary proceedings against employees who have conducted themselves inappropriately on WhatsApp?

Does the private nature of WhatsApp conversations mean that employers are powerless to act?

Is there anything an employer can do to prevent or restrict their employees from using WhatsApp inappropriately?" (Unspecified, 2018.)

The issue of privacy is also important because the messages are meant for the recipient and no one else. Anyone who has had many different chats to navigate, especially if a few are pinging at once, will be familiar with the issue of accidently posting a message into the wrong chat. At one previous job, I had a manager who was erratic and emotionally unstable. As well as a main group chat for staff, a WhatsApp subgroup chat was put in place for the entire team except that manager so that we could monitor that manager's mood and get things done without alerting them to anything that could provoke an outburst. I dread to think what would have happened if a message destined for the subgroup had instead been posted in the main work group chat, but as an employee lower down the ladder, it can be difficult to distance yourself from a pre-existing work culture, or even understand at the time why something carried out might not be a good idea. There have been incidences of occurrences in workplaces where groups of male employees have started private WhatsApp groups to share content of a pornographic nature or to rate their female colleagues, such as recent incidences involving male members of the police force. Such conversations can land the employees in question, or potentially even the company those employees work for, in a lot of trouble whether they knew about the existence of the WhatsApp group or not:

"In reality, section 26 of the Equality Act 2010 is applicable in such cases. It states that if one person harasses another for a protected characteristic; if they engage in unwanted conduct that has the purpose or effect of violating dignity; or they create an intimidating, hostile, offensive or degrading environment, it constitutes a breach of the law. There are no words in the legislation that make exceptions for private phones or emails," says Rice-Birchall. "If you violate dignity in the workplace you can be liable, regardless of where it takes place." (Burt, 2018.)

I return to my example of the previous job with the unstable boss. Despite the subgroup being private, there is nothing to stop another employee from showing any of the messages to that boss for whatever reason they felt the need to. Whether this is punishable as the message was shared in a private context is debateable and depends upon the circumstances, but a negative message will definitely harm what might have once been a good working relationship and could end up with someone losing their job.

He Who Shouts the Loudest

The other problem with work group chats are the other people who take part in them. In an office, there are often people who shout the loudest, whether that's about the state of the coffee machine, the right to listen to a very loud radio during working hours or about how great it is to return to the office after a pandemic. Other colleagues can fall into the trap of thinking that those loudest people represent the views of everyone in the office, even though there are likely more colleagues who disagree with the loud colleagues – they just never say anything. The loud colleagues, who are naturally bold and bullish, might also be the people who post the most in the instant messenger group chat and as a result they could dictate the narrative of the conversation, just as they have dictated how people may perceive their opinions to also be the opinions of everyone in the office. It is important to take anything said in a work group chat with caution and be very guarded and careful with your responses. A few sharing the same humour or opinions does not mean that everyone shares the same humour or opinions, so think carefully before sharing that hilarious video or political joke in the chat.

Many companies have a social media policy which may or may not refer to the use of instant messaging apps and it is important to be familiar with this. Sharing a personal phone number with others without permission is also in breach of the GDPR, and employees should have a right not to join a WhatsApp group if they do not want to. The truth is that despite this, many people will naturally not feel comfortable saying so to their employer and feel obliged to be part of the group, even if they do not want to be.

Chapter 6

Chat Etiquette

Group chats have few, if any, established rules. The 'rules' that do exist only exist as unwritten rules which might be abided by out of a fear of causing upset, rather than because they are logical or grounded in basic politeness or common sense. Rather than the unwritten rules being shared among users, people work out their own rules based on their own perceptions and circumstances. The lack of common rules for instant messaging group chats leaves a void which this chapter aims to fill. The rules and advice laid out in the following pages aim to make group chats of all types a more comfortable and enjoyable experience for everyone involved.

By all means, treat this chapter as a rulebook. However, treat it as a very general rulebook, because each group chat should be judged on its own merit. There is always scope to adapt the rules depending upon which group chat you apply them to. For example, if you know everyone in the group chat really well, and there are no hierarchical barriers, such as your colleagues from work or older relatives, you can be more relaxed in your conduct and choice of topics.

The latter part of this chapter will also talk about changes you can make in the First Dimension in order to better manage your smartphone in the First Dimension, and perhaps even how to use it less overall because how we behave in the dimension in which we use a smartphone can affect how we behave in the Third Dimension, the realm of the smartphone.

Rule 1: Ask First

"I am unfortunately driving one of my friends mad by starting a new group every time I want to say or organise something instead of sticking to the same thread. I wondered if that was why another friend left immediately after I started a group to say, 'Merry Christmas', but I did think it was rude not to post first then leave." (Christmasfairy07, 2019.)

The first rule of the group chat should be to ask if someone would like to be added to the group chat before adding them, otherwise, like this Mumsnet user, you will annoy your friends. It should not even need to be said that this should be the case, "especially if you know that they do not want to be in group chats," because it is basic politeness to ask permission before involving other people in anything. The fact that joining a group chat, or any conversation, is a choice is all too often forgotten, and leaving it is also a choice. Unlike in the real world, people cannot easily decline the conversation via physical or verbal means and this choice is all too often taken away from them.

For many events, such as hen or stag parties, big birthday bashes and even keeping in touch with your children's school, an instant messaging group is now par for the course. It is fine to decide that a group chat is where information for a particular event will be shared, but perhaps bear it in mind that this is not necessarily the way in which people would choose to receive their information. It is polite to have another option where information can be distributed without the additional extras that a group chat can bring.

Rule 2: Keep the Group Chat on Topic

Every instant messaging group chat starts for a reason, and this should not be forgotten. This is not always easy because the longer the chat exists, the harder this will be as conversations change and evolve. "Like the dreaded 'reply all' on an office-wide email, the group chat can quickly go from an effective way to communicate to a large group of friends to a time-consuming worm hole of 'liking' and replying to inane comments that are miles from the topic which sparked the initial conversation." (Izzo, 2020.)

If the group chat is to continue for the sake of continuation, it could inevitably become a dumping group for whatever comes into our minds, no matter how irrelevant or quantitative that might be. If people have joined a group to keep up to date with the arrangements of Benny's Big Benidorm Bash, they will want to be part of a conversation that discusses the event in question, and they probably will not want the group to keep pinging with photos of your children posing on every piece of apparatus in the playground from every angle. Irrelevant information can cause participants to become disengaged, and as Bakhshi says, not only can this be a difficult thing to spot, but once people are disengaged that engagement can be difficult to rebuild:

"In a digital messaging environment, it's much more difficult to spot the moment someone disengages. The previous clues from our physical world disappear. Gone is the visible absence, the body language and even tone of voice. These signs mean that not only is it harder to spot a lack of engagement, but once it is gone, it even more difficult to rebuild." (Bakhshi, 2020.)

To prevent disengagement, pause every so often for a mental check. Is the subject you are discussing relevant to everyone or interesting? Are you perhaps talking about something a little too much? Your recent holiday, new baby or wedding might be a source of joy for you (and rightly so), but that is not all that other people in the group are going to want to hear about. In addition to this, as well as paying attention to what you are saying, also pay attention to what others respond to and how they respond to different messages.

Are you talking to everyone? It might begin unintentionally, but when you begin talking to another chat participant or a few participants about something that is not relevant to most people in the group, such as the party that only some of you are attending that Saturday or unintelligible in-jokes, it is time to tell the relevant participants that you will continue the conversation in a regular chat with just the two of you. Always remember that you are having a conversation with everyone involved. Instant messaging conversations are not the same as a static social media profile page such as Facebook or Instagram, so do not only send messages about yourself, but take care to reply to other people's messages too. If you only talk about the things that are exciting to you, the group chat ceases to become a conversation.

You should also look out for any silences. A silence could mean nothing because outside of the bubble of the group chat, people will be doing other things and may not respond to group chat messages straight away. Any number of things could be happening in the real world to make someone put down their phone suddenly or to disconnect. But if the silence continues for a week or two, and then the group chat comes to life again with the discussion of something completely different, and this happens repeatedly, perhaps you should reconsider withholding some information about a subject which has made you a bit too excited. Let someone else talk for a change.

Going off-topic can also mean that the objectives of the group chat are not met. A friend once recalled the time he was part of a group chat for a stag party. The best man was supposed to organise the stag party. However, despite dumping everyone into a WhatsApp group chat, the best man did not take the lead but instead asked everyone else what they thought the stag party should consist of. For a couple of months, the participants in the chat debated where they should go for the stag party as the flight prices rose and the date neared. This was a waste of time and tiring for all involved. In the end, another fed up chat participant took charge. He just chose a destination, named a price, told everyone what the activities were and booked a hotel. Job done!

Rule 3: Keep Disagreements Out of the Group Chat

Disagreements are a very good reason to take a discussion away from the group. They can quickly escalate even more than they need to as other people, who have watched the argument unfold, can also end up becoming involved unnecessarily. At the most extreme end, just as in the real world, an angry mob can even form:

"Some of the children [in my children's school] are about to take a grammar school test next week and certain parents are up in arms about the teacher upsetting their children by expecting too much off them? Raising her voice and therefore potentially causing them to fail their exams. I personally have no issues with the teacher and didn't when my older son was a pupil there last year.

The messages about this teacher started last week with a lot of parents piling on and ripping her character to shreds. I thought it would blow over and didn't really want to get involved so kept my head down and didn't comment either way.

However within the last few days the messages have taken quite a nasty turn, one parent in particular seems hell bent on rallying the troops to get this teacher out, she has accused the teacher of gross misconduct, emotional abuse and is threatening legal action." (LondonElle, 2021.)

Even if no one else gets involved, arguments taking place among a group can also be very uncomfortable for others to witness, such as O'Kane's example of witnessing his friend being kicked out of a group chat after a breakup. Other arguments can even be entertaining to witness if a participant is far removed from it:

"I died of laughter when in our whatsapp group chat someone wrote 'fuck off Gemma' as a joke about a girl who was doing insanely long answers on our lecture and everyone was agreeing and laughing and turns out she was in the group lmao, I was just sat watching the drama." (totential_rigger, 2020.)

Even if the dispute is amusing to you, it could be awkward or insensitive to others who are watching and hurtful to anyone who is (or ends up becoming) directly or indirectly involved. Either agree to disagree and stop that particular discussion or agree to take the conversation somewhere else. Once people are riled up about a subject, focus can easily be lost and things may be said that are not meant, especially as it is so easy to just type whatever you are thinking into the chat very quickly.

Ideally, the host of the group chat, that is, the person who started the chat, should act as a moderator, reminding people to keep the conversation tidy and to intervene when things start to get out of hand. In reality, many group chats have no clear leader, and no one will remember who started the chat, especially when the same chat has been running for God knows how many years. No one regularly checks the list of participants. When it comes to instant messaging conversations, the most important thing is not who started the discussion, but the most memorable things that were said and where the conversation is going next. Within most instant messaging apps there is the function to designate many people as a moderator, meaning that these people are allowed to add participants to a conversation and not a lot else. Perhaps there should be a function that allocates responsibility to one person so that they can take charge of the chat, not only in cases of disagreements but also to ensure that the chat is relevant and that it does not descend into pointless banter. At the time of writing, the author is not aware of an instant messenger that has such a function, but the ability to allow a chat host to take the lead could be very useful. Perhaps, if any app developers are reading this, consider that there should be some sort of very visible badge or symbol next to a chat host as a reminder that they are the person designated with the task of keeping the group chat in order.

Rule 4: Consider Other Chat Participants
Rule number four is to consider how the subjects that you want to talk to the group about could affect the people who you are talking to.

One thing that happens time and time again is when chat participants make other people in a group chat feel uncomfortable as they send an extravagant thank you to one person in the group chat. Group chats can be an easy place to thank others and to celebrate good deeds and nice gestures. No doubt a friend who is part of a group chat will have done something nice for you at some point. Perhaps a couple of friends did something nice for you. Unless the gesture was a combined one from everyone who is participating in the group chat, or that one friend did the same good gesture for everyone in the chat, you should message each friend separately to say thank you. That way, Diana will not feel like her handmade birthday card is inferior to Katie's champagne hamper, and other participants in the group chat who did not know it was your birthday will not be worrying that they have not bought you anything.

It is perfectly okay to mention your sponsored half marathon in a group chat, but out of courtesy only mention it once, and if you have not told the whole chat that you are doing a half marathon, perhaps thank your wonderful donors separately in a different chat one-on-one. In First Dimension conversations, studies show that the person speaking will avoid imposing any kind of obligation on their listeners because it is uncomfortable for them. The speakers themselves are aware that they would also feel uncomfortable should they also be placed in a situation where they felt obliged to accept an obligation. David Crystal notes that more obligations are imposed on participants in online conversations than in the First Dimension and in addition to this, direct questions, i.e. yes or no questions, are more commonly used online, even if they might be softened by emojis and emoticons. (Crystal, 2020.) This is almost certainly a result of those non-verbal markers (body language, facial expressions, tone of voice, etc.) being absent from online conversations. This further indicates how much we rely on a lot more than words to remind us how to behave towards each other. Another theory for this increase in yes or no questions could be that we do not feel as shy to ask something of others when we are virtually distanced from them, again because we do not have to look them in the eye. Whatever the reason, when taking part in a group chat on an instant messenger, you should make a greater effort to be more aware of what you are saying and how you are saying it.

As well as considering what could make other group chat participants uncomfortable, it is also important to consider the sensitivities of others in the group, especially if you do not know them well. Remember the group's purpose and do not fall into the trap of joining in with a conversation just because the loudest participants are discussing it – they might also unknowingly be causing offence or saying things that other people would prefer not to hear. Stick to the subject and avoid topics such as religion, politics, gender, and anything else that can generally cause people to be upset unless you know the other chat participants really well. Also bear people's possible relationships with others in mind. For example, it is rude to take the lead on discussing the ex-partner of someone who is part of the group chat.

Each participant can help themselves, and others, by setting some rules for themselves. You cannot predict what other people will talk about, and you cannot change other people's behaviour, but you can decide 'if subject X comes up in a group chat, I will not respond' or 'I will not talk about subjects X, Y, Z in a particular group chat'. By doing this, you then at least reduce the risk of getting into a situation that you did not intend to be a part of, and you will not be contributing to any disorder arising from it.

Then there are those conversations that just become plain annoying. What counts as annoyance varies as much as the length of a piece of string. How annoying is annoying and how long will it last? A couple doting on each other – this is likely to pass. A bossy, bragging parent in your child's school WhatsApp group – their irritating presence is likely to last in the group much, much longer.

Remember, you do not always have to reply. You can wait a few days and then change the subject or deflect their comments with humour. Part of the problem with WhatsApp group chats is that too much goes unsaid. If you are included in a group chat, you are as much a part of the conversation as everyone else. If the conversation becomes unsavoury, there is nothing wrong with sending a polite but firm message to let the group know that you would rather some things were not posted in the chat.

Rule 5: Remember to Engage with People in the First Dimension Too

Make sure you engage with friends outside of the group chat and actively seek to do this. If you only engage with friends inside a group chat, this could dilute your relationship. If you only engage with people who you do not know so well inside a group chat, you might never really become friends but only interact with each other within the context of that group. Take the time to talk to the people you care about in private chats individually, and do not forget to spend quality time together in the real world, or at least attempt to invite your friend to do this.

Rule 6: Do Not Take Anything Personally

Never take it personally if someone leaves a group chat, and do not pressure anyone to rejoin. Do not assume that you know why anyone left the group chat and certainly do not create a reason just to fill in the blanks. A participant's reason for leaving is theirs alone and probably does not apply to you personally. If you are worried about a person who has left a group chat, by all means send them a message, but make sure there are no strings attached. Even if you do not find their departure from the group chat to be a big deal, it is nice to message them anyway. They will probably be very happy that you thought to contact them personally and your friendship will be stronger for it.

Managing Group Chats in the Real World

Smartphone use transcends the barrier between the real and virtual words because we use our phone in the First Dimension and therefore, in order to establish and maintain good chat etiquette within the virtual realm, we cannot only consider actions that can be carried out in the Third Dimension. There are many things that you can do in the First Dimension in order to manage your smartphone in the Third Dimension better. The following suggestions could even help you to use your smartphone less overall.

Rule 7: Limit, Limit, Limit

"Research has shown that problematic smartphone usage is related to the frequency of usage as well as to the amount of time spent on the phone. In this rather unsurprising context, problematic smartphone usage is defined by the fact that people spend so much time with their phone that this may have a negative impact on user's health, on their body posture and respiratory functions, on academic and cognitive performances and on users' psychological wellbeing leading to symptoms of depression." (Catharina Münch, 2020.)

This quote nicely illustrates some of the problems which can arise when smartphones are used too much, and no one would deny that they are frequently used for many hours a day by their users – us. The smartphone is a tiny computer that is never far from our thoughts. For many, it is the wake-up call in the morning and the last thing we look at night before falling asleep – that is, if you can turn it off and are able to go to sleep at all. Physical symptoms, such as bad body posture, aside, group chats, as we have discussed, can be a source of stress and anxiety, and the same can be said for the smartphone itself. There can be a chain reaction if someone is not in a great state of mind when using a smartphone. That person is likely to overshare or to communicate things that could cause others to feel stressed, then in turn others may communicate their own stresses in another chat. When in a poor state of mind, you are also more likely to send messages that you did not mean to send. So, rule seven is all about limiting yourself, your contacts and your smartphone access. Understandably, self-control can be difficult when you are stressed but confiding your stresses in one or a few select friends or family members could be more beneficial to yourself and others rather than confiding all of your woes in a group chat.

As well as limiting your smartphone use overall, there are also physical things you can do in order to limit how often you access groups chats and apps. These in turn will help you to limit your smartphone engagements in general. When put into practice, this will not just relieve the stress that you feel from feeling obliged to monitor many group conversations, but it will improve your mental health and well-being overall too. By limiting how often we use our phones in the real world, we can also improve our phone usage in the virtual world. If we engage with group chats less often, we will in turn converse less within them and perhaps be more mindful of what we contribute to them.

One place to start is by creating phone-free zones or phone-free times. Keeping the phone out of the bedroom would be a good place to begin. Alarm clocks come in all shapes and sizes and there are many affordable devices on the market. Another important ritual that deserves not to involve a phone is when you eat meals, whether with the family, friends or alone. If you have children, it is especially important that they have your full attention and the chance to interact with you at mealtimes in order to both develop their own social skills and to feel secure in the knowledge that Mum and Dad and any other caregivers they depend on are there for them. In addition, according to Turkle, "we use conversations with each other to learn how to have conversations with ourselves. So a flight from conversation can really matter because it can compromise our capacity for self-reflection. For kids growing up, that skill is the bedrock of development." (Turkle, 2012.)

An hour or two before bed is another time when it is good to wind down without the pesky smartphone. We have already mentioned sleep, and screens are notorious for disrupting the essential process of switching off. This is because the blue light generated by devices disrupts the production of melatonin, the hormone that keeps your circadian rhythm (otherwise known as the body clock) in check, and without it you wake up and find it harder to doze off. It is also worth staying away from your smartphone during the night. If you are on your phone, you will almost certainly look at your messages. Because the topics of discussion in a group chat can be stressful or exciting, checking the group chat can heighten your senses just as you need them to relax. Physically putting your smartphone in a drawer or a cupboard at a specified time might be one way of using your phone less. "Out of sight, out of mind" – it is a saying as old as time, but it really does work.

You could go even further and take the leap to reduce your phone use overall. If your phone is your constant companion, or you require it for work, this might be easier said than done. The advice here would be to reduce the time that you spend on your phone very gradually. Even engaging with your phone for five minutes less at a time is a good start. If restricting your phone use is a challenge, limiting the times that you look at instant messaging groups can also make them easier to deal with. It is recommended that you "only participate in any WhatsApp group once a day and not first thing in the morning or last thing at night. You do not wish to start your day feeling anxious or try and go to asleep anxious". (Moss, 2020.)

Rule 8: Tone Down

Changing your phone from having a colourful façade to being in greyscale (or black and white) is also said to reduce smartphone use overall, some sources even going as far as to say that greyscale can be a cure for smartphone addiction. Calling this tactic a 'cure-all' might be debatable, but what a greyscale screen does do is take away the cues which encourage our brains, and ultimately ourselves, to keep engaging with the device. You can change your phone façade to greyscale in the main settings, although on some older smartphones this might not be so simple, and you may have to activate the developer mode. It may or may not require a bit of effort but is worth a try.

Smartphone apps are designed to have a 'trigger, action, reward' system which works in the same way that slot machines function. The bright colours, along with the pop-up notifications and the noises that accompany them, are part of this design. They are intended to grab and keep hold of your attention and it does not take a genius to work out that these features were not added to your smartphone by accident. Therefore, changing the colour of your phone to greyscale will be a more effective if app notifications are turned off too.

It is possible to mute group chats indefinitely within WhatsApp so that notifications do not just appear on your phone. However, these have to be done one by one which can take time if you have multiple conversations open. If you are someone who checks the app a bit too regularly, this method may not make much difference as to how you interact with WhatsApp, or how the app might make you feel. A more effective method, which works regardless of the instant messaging app that you use, is to stop group chats, and other chats, just popping up at random. To do this you can turn off the app's ability to send pop-up notifications to your phone entirely in your notification settings. This option is usually found under your smartphone's main settings, most likely under 'notifications management' or a similar title. As you are in the settings, it is worthwhile turning off app notifications for almost every, if not every, app in order to reduce your phone's ability to call out for your attention.

Rule 9: Use the Broadcast Function

I will let you in on a little secret. If you want to message a few people at once, but do not want the hassle of a group chat, WhatsApp has a little-known, and little-used, broadcast function. This function allows you to select a number of people to receive a single message without any of the recipients knowing that anyone else has received the same message as them. WhatsApp says that this feature can be used to contact up to 256 participants at once but warns that maxing out the feature may cause some messages to be delayed. Once the messages are sent via this function, they will either go to an existing chat that you already have open with a person or open a new chat with a person. You can also track the messages you have sent in the broadcast chat box, which is marked by a megaphone symbol.

To use the broadcast function on WhatsApp (Android):
1. WhatsApp > More Options (aka the Hamburger Menu) > New broadcast
2. Search for or select the contacts you want to add
3. Write a message
4. Send your message

To use the broadcast feature on WhatsApp (iPhone):
1. Tap Broadcast Lists at the top of the Chats screen
2. Tap New List at the bottom of the Broadcast Lists screen
3. Search for or select the contacts you want to add
4. Tap Create

This function could be very useful, and a lot less stressful, for people who are organising events for big groups such as hen dos and parties. It could also be useful for work groups because you can convey information quickly to individual participants without any obligation for them to enter into a group chat. The conversation will be restricted to the two of you, thus leaving no scope for unwanted chit-chat.

To Summarise
The smartphone is very far removed from the phone it originated from. Far from being a basic receiver with a solely numerical keypad left in the corner of the living room or hanging on a roadside inside a large metal box, it is a tiny computer that we spend most of our waking lives engaging with. The technology is relatively new, and it mentally and visually transports us from one dimension to another. It takes us from actual reality to virtual reality, leaving the essential material things that we need to be able to communicate with each other in an optimal manner behind. We could really, really do with taking these essential human elements into the Third Dimension with us, but in their absence, we can set rules and boundaries for ourselves that will in turn improve our awareness and help us to retain common sense and a sense of perspective.

Take your time when putting these rules into practice and do not expect miracles to happen overnight. Gradually you should find that instant messaging conversations should become easier and more pleasant. You cannot make others change their behaviour. However, when you change your own behaviour, people may have to adjust theirs accordingly. People are copycats and gradually behavioural change may happen as a result of mass imitation. Once people relax and become more considerate of others in the group chat, it should become a better experience for everyone involved.

Chapter 7

Leaving the Group Chat

"Rules and identities provide a basis for decision making in every aspect of life: in families, informal groups, markets, political campaigns, and revolutions. Individuals and social systems depend on rules and on the standardisation, routinisation, and organisation of actions that they provide. From this perspective, a decision in any context can be seen as being shaped by identities and a logic of appropriateness." (March, 1994.)

In life we are constantly having to justify our choices. If I want two weeks off from work on a particular date, I do not want to sign up for a service or I do not want to wear a particular outfit for a formal occasion, it is never enough to just tell another person that the reason that I do or do not want to do these things is simply because I do or do not want to. I can guarantee you that there will have been lots of times that you have had to make up excuses just so that the other person stops asking why, when really the truth is that there is no other reason than you just do not want to and, as a person with free will, that should be enough. Despite this, if your reason was not convincing enough, you would likely have been met with a complaint about a poor excuse. But if you were only able to express that you did not want to do whatever it was in the first place, you would not have had to pretend that there was a reason why.

In the same vein, it should be easy to leave any conversation because you just want to, when you have said all that you have to say, and you do not have a reason to remain. But as is human nature, many people will not accept this decision.

In most cases no one questions why we leave a chat in the First Dimension because either our non-verbal cues have already announced that we are no longer taking part and why, or because the other person or people who we are talking to can also see that the chat has served its purpose and therefore the conversation can end through an unspoken yet mutual agreement. But this is often not the case in the Third Dimension. Leaving the group chat in the digital realm can even be seen as an aggressive act, even if you just do not feel that your presence is warranted, and that the conversation is not adding anything positive to your life.

Oh No, You Are Leaving!

It is an interesting paradox that many of us want to leave groups chats, but, at the same time the thought of others leaving fills us with dread. Opinions on leaving group chats are shaped by personal perspectives and perceptions of what is deemed appropriate and as a result, they from vary widely from individual to individual as the following quotes from a Quora thread from 2021 illustrate:

"From a personal experience, I leave, left, would leave a WhatsApp group if I find most of the members are quiet. Then there is no point to be in a group with people who are not contributing." (Motsoane, 2021.)

"I never liked people who left a group without leaving a message. It's like getting up from a table full of people without so much as an 'excuse me.'" (Margabandhu, 2018.)

"It takes a brave person to exit [an instant messaging group chat]." (Rameshwar, 2021.)

"This situation [leaving a WhatsApp group] is giving me serious anxiety and I'm losing sleep. When I used to see them, I was the butt of jokes, my clothes, hair… they made me feel like they didn't respect me so I stopped seeing them. I tried to leave quietly but got readded. One girl is texting me asking why I left." (Lewis, 2019.)

Why would our decision to leave a digital group chat raise questions or assumptions? To better understand this, let's return to what seems to be a human need to justify our choices. The reason that this need exists could be because by asking something of someone, be it working on a particular date, accepting an invitation to a party or requesting an outfit to be worn for a particular occasion, the person wanting such things to be done has a goal, and if you like that person and want to please them, or you are lower on the hierarchy and expected to obey them (such as in the workplace or within the family structure), society says that you should not object to such requests and you should help the other person achieve that goal. At some level the decision not to oblige is seen as personal, even if it actually is not. If you cannot give a good reason why you cannot honour their request, it means in turn that the person making the request feels negative and they are entitled to feel this way. The need to justify decisions and choices is internalised, both by the people who expect something from someone, and by the people who are deciding whether to honour the request.

The act of leaving an instant messaging group chat fits into this narrative. On the surface, being part of a group chat seems like a small gesture that does not require much effort or inconvenience, and we might put up with this supposedly small inconvenience and the negative things that come with it in order to please others. The negative aspects of the chat might even be cancelled out by the positive aspects of being on good terms with others and perhaps even benefitting from the nice conversations and any social invitations that arise from them – at least in the beginning.

With a lack of clarification for another person's actions, we might find it hard to accept that someone has left a group chat and why they might have done that. Accepting that they might have left it just because they wanted to goes against what makes us human. The fact that human beings are always searching for reasons for everything, even when there is no reason, makes group chat participants feel that even if they did politely say that they were leaving the group chat, nobody would believe them and everyone else would reach their own conclusion, as some of the comments from the Quora forum illustrate. This could mean that anyone leaving a group chat could be impacted negatively by their decision to leave the group chat, and this is in itself enough of a reason to stay.

The More You Know

What is definite is that a group chat is much easier to leave if you do not know the people in the group very well, because the consequences of doing so are not as great for you. The unique event group, such as the hen or stag party group, is likely to be populated by group chat participants that you do not know, and once the event is over there is nothing to stop you from leaving that group chat. It is almost guaranteed that everyone else will do the same.

In groups where you know the participants well, or you might have a very close friend or two, leaving the instant messaging group chat can be much harder because the decision to leave will have an effect on the other chat participants as well as your guilty conscience. If you are close to someone who remains in the group chat, that person might feel hurt that you do not want to participate in something they consider to be fun and a shared bonding experience. If the chat is the only way that you have a bond with any one participant who has left, their departure could effectively sever that bond and the thought of a bond being severed, no matter how remote the relationship, can be very unsettling, even though this feeling might be temporary. When the other participants are people that you do not know too well but are people that you have to bond with out of circumstance, such as other parents from your children's year at school who you will likely see face-to-face in the near future, you might stay to save face. How leaving the chat can affect the other participants, and oneself, can be another deterrent from leaving.

With so much at stake, how on earth does anyone leave a group chat?

How to Leave a Group Chat

In an ideal world, leaving a group chat would not even be a topic of discussion but unfortunately it is. The act of doing so is hard, and we have gone through the reasons why this can be. When the time comes to leave the group chat for whatever reason you may or may not have, before you do anything else, write a nice, neutral, brief message to let the participants know what you will do. Psychologist Jacqui Manning from New South Wales, Australia recommends writing the following message (or something similar) before leaving in order to soften the blow:

"Something along the lines of 'I'm cleaning up on my screen use and realise I need to streamline my social media and chat groups, so I've decided it's best for me to leave this chat. Will see you soon at work/school/next family function' whatever is relevant." (Izzo, 2020.)

This message is neutral and concise, bringing the focus onto what you need, stating that you do not want to cut anyone off and you welcome anyone who wants to contact you to be able to do so. There is no guarantee that questions won't be asked regarding your departure, and you will not be pulled back into a group, but at least you have not just disappeared without a reason.

Then you can physically leave the group chat by carrying out the following steps within WhatsApp:

1. Select the group chat that you want to leave
2. Select the Hamburger Menu
3. Select More
4. Exit Group
5. Yes

Congratulations, you left the group. The conversation will still be on your phone, but you can easily delete it by selecting it and clicking on the bin (trash can) symbol.

The Aftermath

Until recently, when a participant left a WhatsApp group chat, a message would pop up that stated that that participant had left the chat. The message is in itself a glaring indication that someone has decided to leave and opens up the floor to opinions and theories. Reports began circulating in early 2022 that WhatsApp was working on a feature that would allow chat participants to leave a group chat silently. This feature, at the time of writing, has only just been released and it is therefore yet to be seen how good or helpful it will be. Even if no message now shows when you leave a group chat, there is no doubt that leaving the chat on the app is just the first step. Even if a minimal number of people know about your departure, the chat will still be in your list of conversations, complete with the entire chat history, until you purposely delete it. Looking back at the chat could evoke emotions about the fact that you have left a group chat and could make leaving the next group chat harder.

As for the other participants, even if you leave silently, they will realise that you are no longer taking part sooner or later. The other chat participants will probably ask where you are and ask the others why you are no longer part of the chat (which, if your partner or someone very close to you is still in the chat, could cause them to feel awkward). They will likely then proceed to message you and try to convince you to join again. The other participants might even omit that step and add you back in without trying to ask you why, until the chat is back on your phone and you're bombarded with messages asking where you went and why you left.

Ignorance is Bliss

WhatsApp has settings that allow you to mute chats regardless of how many other people are taking part. This is an option if you do not feel ready to go through leaving a chat. In reality, muting a chat does not mean that you will not see the messages in the various group chats on your phone when you do look at it, and my bet is that you are checking your phone regularly. Ignorance might provide some relief, but you still know that the messages will be there.

How to Mute a Group Chat

To stop overly active group chats notifying you of anything that is added to them:

1. Open WhatsApp
2. Select WhatsApp group
3. Hamburger Menu
4. Mute Notifications
5. Select the duration (I select Always)
6. Click Okay

This is very handy for groups that you check less, because even the numbers marker will not show up. But the most recently active conversation will still appear at the top of your chat list, and if you are someone who checks WhatsApp a lot, this function does not deter you from checking any conversation on your list numerous times.

Prevention is Better than a Cure

There are also settings to prevent yourself being added to a group chat in the first place, which could at least stop you being caught up in conversations with less familiar people.

How to prevent yourself from being added to a WhatsApp group chat:

1. Account
2. Privacy
3. Groups
4. Who Can Add Me to Groups
5. Select who can add you, which at the time of writing is Everyone, My Contacts or My Contacts Except, which allows you to block certain people.

Whoever you block using the method above can send you a private message to ask if they can add you to a group chat, but they cannot simply add you into a chat at once without your permission.

Remove pop-up notifications

You can also remove pop-up notifications so that you are less tempted to look at your phone. In theory, this is helpful, and it is, at least a little. When you cannot see that someone has messaged you, and what the message contains, it makes the phone slightly less slot machine-like.

How to remove pop-up notifications from
WhatsApp (Android):
1. WhatsApp
2. Hamburger Menu
3. Settings
4. Notifications
5. Groups
6. Set Pop-up notification to No pop-up
7. Set Use High Priority Notifications to off

How to remove pop-up notifications from
WhatsApp (iPhone):
1. WhatsApp > Settings
2. Click on Notifications
3. Under Group Notifications turn off Show Notifications

Reducing the Importance of the Group Chat

Think back to the days when you were a child. Remember how it was to be in the playground. You would climb up the steps to use the slide, probably behind a queue of other children. The children would use the slide in different ways and one cool kid might go down the slide backwards. Seeing them do that, you copy them. Then you might go down the slide stopping halfway down by rubbing the soles of your shoes on the metal, the other child notices and docs the same. A connection is formed. You play in the sandpit together and a third child helps you build an impressive sandcastle. It is uneven and falls down suddenly, but that does not matter. You are a team now. You exchange names and talk about all sorts of things, including the task at hand.

As we grow older, most people lose this ability to strike up a conversation so easily and effortlessly, becoming more self-conscious, judgemental, and even suspicious of each other. We are too tired and too busy to make friends so easily and we worry that people will not like us back. Yet relearning this skill can pay off, and, in theory, should be easy to do, if not easier, in the semi-anonymous environment of the instant messaging group chat. You might not want to talk to everyone in the hen party group, but you notice that one participant is a bit more reserved but seems keen to advocate for the horse trek as a morning activity. You like horse riding too. You message her privately because you have something in common and it would be good to have a friend at the event because the only other person you know, the bride-to-be, will have a lot to juggle. The reserved horse fan is responsive and as you talk to someone you actually feel a connection with you find yourself paying less attention to the group.

It is worth remembering that you do have the option on an instant messaging app to interact with your friends in a regular chat instead of replying to them (and everyone else) in the group chat. If you stick to this rule, you could eventually make the group become redundant and with a base of strong bonds established between yourself and the people you care about, it might feel easier to leave. Like your child self in the playground all those years ago – you can also make friends with people in the First Dimension too.

Re-Entering the Instant Messaging Group Conversation

Leaving any instant messaging group does not have to be final, but any re-entry should always be on your terms. If you have set up some of the settings mentioned above, this should be enough to stop you simply being pulled back into the WhatsApp group.

Depending on the circumstances of the departure, if someone leaves your group chat you could always message that person and ask if they want to be invited back in the group. If they do not, then that is okay. Alternatively, leave them be. They probably just did not want to be part of the conversation any longer, and that is completely okay.

To Conclude

Who would have predicted that something which was created to make doing business easier would have become such a huge part of our everyday lives? It is hard to believe now that many telecom companies even regarded the text message in the beginning as nothing special and did not charge for sending them. Instant messengers, and in particular WhatsApp, have been described as 'the heart of the smartphone' and the group chat has become the default mode of communication for people of all ages because it caters very well for different circumstances and scenarios that exist in their everyday lives. In a short space of time, we have entered into a digital age that will only continue to advance and become even more digital. Even whilst writing this book, apps and devices have been updated, new smartphones have been released, companies are falling over themselves to go viral on TikTok, AI chatbots have been added to Snapchat and the metaverse might be on the horizon. There have been many updates to every platform and many more updates will no doubt be released before this book is finally published. That, however, does not mean that we need to use a group chat for everything.

Due to the sheer pace of these developments, it is very important that we seek to understand the new technologies that we are using as they evolve and what they should or should not be used for. This understanding will set us in good stead to be able to establish ground rules that we can apply to applications such as instant messengers and group chats so that we can use them comfortably and be prepared for how they may affect ourselves and others. We also need to learn how to navigate communications as they function within different dimensions and cross them so that we are not overwhelmed, and we can keep sight of our priorities.

How Technology Has Affected Us

Instant messenger group chats have both positive and negative aspects to them and so they have affected us and our communication habits in good and bad ways. If they were entirely negative, they would never have become as widely used and popular as they are today, and they certainly would never have become considered 'the heart of the smartphone'. We enjoy taking part in group conversations wherever they may take place, and so we should. Whether virtually or in-person, there are a lot of benefits for us when we engage with other people because we are naturally social creatures. Digital group conversations can make communicating with lots of people in different places quicker and easier and we benefit from the virtual support and companionship that we get from them. On the flip side, these conversations can also be overwhelming, annoying and we might not have asked or wanted to take part in them. We can very quickly end up with too many groups to keep track of – some of them including people we might not like – and be constantly connecting with more people than we evolved to handle and receive more messages than we are able to read.

Social media has largely levelled the technological playing field for different age groups who are now all being exposed to, and engaging in, the same things. As a result of this, the boundaries of adults and children have been blurred like never before. Constantly communicating with others has brought joys, as well as issues of helicopter parenting and inevitable clashes that come from being in contact with certain people too often. The group chat can continue forever in the Third Dimension and, because the motives behind our words and actions are not so clear, chat participants can feel uncomfortable when other participants try to leave and be afraid to leave the group chat themselves. If anyone does leave, there can be mass panic or even drama. To avoid any drama, we inconvenience ourselves for the sake of others by staying and so the cycle continues. There is no reason why anyone should feel so uncomfortable about leaving a group chat that they would make a choice to remain in the conversation for the sake of it and feel stressed while doing so. This book was written to explore how and why we have ended up feeling this way so that this could be changed. You might feel more confident now, or you might need to reread some of the chapters before you are able to make decisions concerning the conversations that you do and do not want to take part in. This book is that helping hand, your permission to make a choice – to stay or to leave. This book is your reassurance that whatever you choose, everything will be fine.

Established Rules Can Help Us Communicate in a More Positive Way

The negative aspects of instant messengers and group chats are not entirely caused by the medium itself – an instant messenger is after all only a digital interface which allows us to send messages and not much more. It is the behaviours and beliefs that we, and others, have when using the medium which cause issues, but these are not always our fault. Due to their set-up, the perception we have of the chats we are in is a personal and somewhat private one – we each have our own opinions regarding how both we and everyone else should behave in them and these perceptions do not always align. Following established rules would mean that many of the negative aspects of instant messengers might no longer be an issue or even exist at all which would make participating in them less annoying and stressful. They would help us to feel more confident communicating in the Third Dimension, and to feel more positive about group chats. If there are written rules that we can follow, and we know that other people are also largely following, we would have a collective, rather than an isolated, understanding of group chats and a clearer idea of our role within them. They would establish a common ground which is currently missing from many group chats.

When many of our natural real-world conversational markers are absent, being able to abide by rules gives us back that sense of safety and predictability which is currently largely missing from many digital social interactions. Written rules can keep us on the same page as everyone else. They help remind us to adopt certain common courtesies such as asking first before adding people to a chat and keeping any arguments or issues out of a chat when they do not belong there. Rules can also be personal to us, slowing our conversation down so that we are less prone to saying something which could be perceived as offensive or problematic and allowing us to adopt a disciplined approach to our smartphone use which can help us physically as well as mentally. Rules make us more mindful of how we communicate and subsequently allow us to communicate better with each other.

Communication Begins, and Must Continue, in the Real World

Communication via an instant messenger takes place in the Third Dimension and this is always important to remember. To gain a thorough understanding of how we communicate within the Third Dimension (dimensions being definitions that were created for the purpose of categorising our communications), and why we communicate the way we do, we looked at how instant messengers, social media and technological devices have changed the way that we communicate with each other together, allowing us to become mentally immersed in the digital world as well as accessible at all times. We noted how this new way of communicating is quite different from how we would communicate in the First Dimension, that is, in the real world with each other naturally as human beings – in our default state. Communicating one-to-one (or one-to-a-few) with other people in the real world is where we communicate most comfortably and where we gain the greatest understanding of what is meant when someone speaks. In the Second and Third Dimensions we have had to adapt our ways of communicating in order to navigate each of the new communicational challenges that have arisen as the different technologies have been used for this purpose. Despite becoming more comfortable with the changes in the way we communicate via these new technologies, we still experience a degree of stress when we do so because we cannot use what is naturally at hand: our bodies, voices, and expressions. Once we understand this, not only are we able to understand where any potential communicational problems or conflicts could lie, which in of itself could be reassuring, but, although not everything is possible, we can draw upon the way in which we would communicate in the First Dimension as a basis for how we can communicate in the Third Dimension. This should make us better at communicating with others. Just as in the real world, it is okay to slow down, consider how to answer and not to respond instantly at all times of day, it is fine to just talk to one person instead of an entire group, and the conversation does not have to last forever.

It is also important to ensure that we continue to communicate and contact others in the real world so that we can retain those bonds with the people we care about and, above all, be human. Do not rely too heavily on messaging chats but also call people and make an effort to meet up in-person in the real world, and when you are with them, be present. Communication can easily cross the different dimensions, but, just as in the example of my friend's mother on the telephone when she was talking both on the phone and telling off her children at the same time, we should communicate within one dimension at a time and choose to converse within the one that is most appropriate at the given time.

And Finally

Writing this book has been one long conversation in itself. Everyone I have spoken to about the project has had something to say about the issue – whether they have been affected by the issues covered, know a great story about someone else that is related to this topic or whether they are self-confessed technophobes who do not much care for group chats and never use them. Like all good conversations, this one must come to an end for now, but the discussion about instant messengers and group chats is only just getting started.

References

Agger, B. (2015). Oversharing: Presentations of Self in the Internet Age. United Kingdom: Routledge.

Allthebiscuits. (2019, July 17). Mumsnet: To be annoyed by WhatsApp Group Chats. Retrieved from https://www.mumsnet.com: https://www.mumsnet.com/Talk/am_i_being_unreasonable/3641073-To-be-annoyed-by-WhatsApp-group-chats

Anderson, C. M., & Myers, S. A. (2008). The Fundamentals of Small Group Communication. In The Fundamentals of Small Group Communication (p.284). SAGE Publications.

Arthur, C. (2012, December 03). Text messages turns 20 – but are their best years behind them? Retrieved from The Guardian: https://www.theguardian.com/technology/2012/dec/02/text-messaging-turns-20

Bakhshi, H. (2020, May 28). What our family WhatsApp group can teach us about team communication. Retrieved March 05, 2021, from https://www.linkedin.com/: https://www.linkedin.com/pulse/what-our-family-whatsapp-group-can-teach-us-team-hema-bakhshi/?articleId=6671434615082766336

Bennett, R. (2020, January 13). Head tells parents to quit WhatsApp groups so pupils learn from errors. Retrieved

March 12, 2021, from https://www.thetimes.co.uk/:
https://www.thetimes.co.uk/article/head-tells-parents-
to-quit-whatsapp-groups-so-pupils-learn-from-errors-
hbsjwf2vq

Burt, E. (2018, May 24). Do you know what your employees
are saying in private messages? Retrieved March 06, 2021,
from https://www.peoplemanagement.co.uk: https://
www.peoplemanagement.co.uk/long-reads/articles/what-
employees-saying-private-messaging-whatsapp-slack#gref

Burtis, John O.; Turman, Paul D. (2005). Group Communication
Pitfalls Overcoming Barriers to an Effective Group
Experience. SAGE Publications.

Catharina Münch, L. F. (2020). Time to Log Off: An Analysis of
Factors Influencing the Willingness to Participate in a Long-
Term 'Digital Detox'. HCI International 2020 – Posters
22nd International Conference, HCII 2020 Copenhagen,
Denmark, July 19–24, 2020 Proceedings, Part III (p.228).
Copenhagen: Springer.

CharDee. (2020, July 14). Group chats getting out of hand.
Retrieved February 14, 2021, from https://www.mumsnet.
com/: https://www.mumsnet.com/Talk/am_i_being_
unreasonable/3967565-group-chats-getting-out-of-
hand?pg=10

Charlie Bloom, L. B. (2017, December 05). Playing Out Our
Childhood Role – How you grow up determines who you
will become. Retrieved from https://www.psychologytoday.
com: https://www.psychologytoday.com/us/blog/stronger-
the-broken-places/201712/playing-out-our-childhood-role

Christmasfairy07. (2019, January 3). Thoughts about Watsapp.
Retrieved from Mumsnet: https://www.mumsnet.com/
talk/_chat/3468895-Thoughts-About-Watsapp

Cooney, G. G. (2020). Do conversations end when people want
them to? Cambridge, MA, USA: PNAS. Retrieved November

2021, from https://www.pnas.org/content/118/10/
e2011809118

Crystal, D. (2020). Let's Talk – How English Conversation
Works. United Kingdom: Oxford University Press.

Crystal, D. (2020). Let's Talk – How English Conversation
Works. United Kingdom: Oxford University Press.

Crystal, D. (2020). Let's Talk How English Conversation Works.
Oxford: Oxford University Press.

Dan Bouhnik, M. D. (2014). WhatsApp Goes to School: Mobile
Instant Messaging between Teachers and Students. Journal
of Information Technology Education: Research, 226.

DSP. (2021, January 09). A Brief History of Skype – the peer to
peer messaging service. Retrieved from dsp.co.uk: https://
content.dsp.co.uk/history-of-skype

Dunbar, R. I. (2015). Do online social media cut through the
constraints that limit the size of offline social networks?
Royal Society Open Sci. Retrieved February 13, 2021,
from https://royalsocietypublishing.org/doi/pdf/10.1098/
rsos.150292

Gander, K. (2017, September 25). What is it with WhatsApp
lurkers? A psychologist on why people linger in group
chats. Retrieved March 02, 2021, from https://www.
independent.co.uk/: https://www.independent.co.uk/life-
style/whatsapp-lurkers-psychologists-people-group-chats-
not-say-message-a7966766.html

Gregersen, E. (2020, March 03). Encyclopedia Britannica.
Retrieved from britannica.com: https://www.britannica.
com/topic/instant-messaging

Guild, T. (2020, February 14). Study: New WhatsApp research
highlights the extent of a 'shadow communications'
business risk. Retrieved March 03, 2021, from https://
guild.co/blog/: https://guild.co/blog/study-whatsapp-
professional-use/

Hassler, C. (2008, 09 26). You And Your Twenty-Something Child: How Close Is Too Close? Retrieved February 28, 2021, from https://www.huffpost.com/: https://www.huffpost.com/entry/you-and-your-twenty-somet_b_121225

ilovearticroll. (2019, October 20). To remove myself from family WhatsApp. Retrieved December 08, 2021, from https://www.mumsnet.com/: https://www.mumsnet.com/Talk/am_i_being_unreasonable/3722640-to-remove-myself-from-family-whatsapp

Izzo, A. (2020, January 16). Use this psychologist's script the next time you want to leave an annoying group chat. Retrieved March 13, 2021, from https://www.bodyandsoul.com.au/: https://www.bodyandsoul.com.au/mind-body/wellbeing/use-this-psychologists-script-the-next-time-you-want-to-leave-an-annoying-group-chat/news-story/c3abd79da55d37f7bc9fc5ce942f11ba

Jr, F. A. (2013, March 21). Ex-conman Frank Abagnale warns how Facebook users risk identity theft. (The Guardian) Retrieved March 10, 2023, from The Guardian (on YouTube): https://www.youtube.com/watch?v=RgYDcnFSzys

Kuhnke, E. (2016). Body Language: Learn How to Read Others and Communicate with Confidence. Chichester, United Kingdom: Capstone.

Lewis, B. (2019, Unknown Unknown). What is your best reason to leave a WhatsApp group? Retrieved January 23, 2022, from Quora: https://www.quora.com/What-is-your-best-reason-to-leave-a-WhatsApp-group

littlemisseatsherfeelings. (2016, October 11). To detest WhatsApp. Retrieved March 22, 2022, from Mumsnet: https://www.mumsnet.com/Talk/am_i_being_unreasonable/2753876-to-detest-whatsapp

Lizzie523. (2020, July 10). To be fed up with these group chats now? Retrieved from https://www.mumsnet.

com: https://www.mumsnet.com/Talk/am_i_being_unreasonable/3964161-To-be-fed-up-with-these-group-chats-now

LondonElle. (2021, September 18). To report a class group chat. Retrieved from Mumsnet: https://www.mumsnet.com/talk/am_i_being_unreasonable/4352415-to-report-a-class-group-chat

Lyons, A. (2020, August 20). WhatsApp groups for new mums are more effective at providing support than NHS services, according to new research. Retrieved from https://www.qmul.ac.uk/media/news/: https://www.qmul.ac.uk/media/news/2020/hss/whatsapp-groups-for-new-mums-are-more-effective-at-providing-support-than-nhs-services-according-to-new-research.html

March, J. G. (1994). A Primer on Decision Making. New York: Free Press.

Margabandhu, R. (2018, Unknown Unknown). What is your best reason to leave a WhatsApp group? Retrieved January 23, 2022, from Quora: https://www.quora.com/What-is-your-best-reason-to-leave-a-WhatsApp-group

Mehrabian, A. (1971). Silent Messages. Belmont California: Wadsworth Publishing.

Miller, D. e. (2021). The Global Smartphone: Beyond a Youth Technology. London: UCL Press. Retrieved 2022

Moss, R. (2020, March 26). Group Chats Making You Anxious? Us, Too. Here's How To Manage Them. Retrieved from https://www.huffingtonpost.co.uk/: https://www.huffingtonpost.co.uk/entry/whatsapp-group-chats-managing-anxiety_uk_5e7b714cc5b62a1870d61db4?guccounter=1&guce_